IN CHRIST'S OWN COUNTRY

by

Rev. Francis E. Clark, D.D., LL. D.

President of the World's
Christian Endeavor Union

Author of Old Homes of New
Americans, The Continent of
Opportunity, Christian
Endeavor in All Lands, Etc.

First Fruits Press
Wilmore, Kentucky
c2015

In Christ's Own Country by Rev. Francis E. Clark, D.D., LL.D.

First Fruits Press, ©2015
Previously published: New York and London : Fleming H. Revell, Company, ©1914.

ISBN: 9781621713494 (print), 9781621713500 (digital)

Digital version at http://place.asburyseminary.edu/firstfruitsheritagematerial/102/

First Fruits Press is a digital imprint of the Asbury Theological Seminary, B.L. Fisher Library. Asbury Theological Seminary is the legal owner of the material previously published by the Pentecostal Publishing Co. and reserves the right to release new editions of this material as well as new material produced by Asbury Theological Seminary. Its publications are available for noncommercial and educational uses, such as research, teaching and private study. First Fruits Press has licensed the digital version of this work under the Creative Commons Attribution Noncommercial 3.0 United States License. To view a copy of this license, visit http://creativecommons.org/licenses/by-nc/3.0/us/.

For all other uses, contact:

First Fruits Press
B.L. Fisher Library
Asbury Theological Seminary
204 N. Lexington Ave.
Wilmore, KY 40390
http://place.asburyseminary.edu/firstfruits

Anderson, R.P., 1877-1967.
   In Christ's Own Country by Rev. Francis E. Clark, D.D., LL.D.
   173 pages ; 21 cm.
   Wilmore, Ky. : First Fruits Press, ©2015.
   Reprint. Previously published: New York ; London : Fleming H. Revell Company,©1914.
   ISBN: 9781621713494 (pbk.)

   1. Holiness. 2. Spiritual life. I. Title. II. Convention for Deepening of Spiritual Life

BV4501 .P38 2015   204

Cover design by Wesley Wilcox

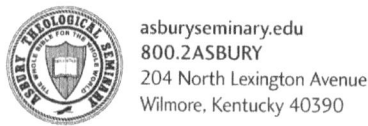

asburyseminary.edu
800.2ASBURY
204 North Lexington Avenue
Wilmore, Kentucky 40390

THE GARDEN OF GETHSEMANE.

IN CHRIST'S OWN COUNTRY

BY

REV. FRANCIS E. CLARK, D. D., LL. D.

President of the World's Christian Endeavor Union

Author of Old Homes of New Americans, The Continent of Opportunity, Christian Endeavor in All Lands, Etc.

THE CHRISTIAN HERALD

BIBLE HOUSE, NEW YORK

Copyright, 1914,
BY
THE CHRISTIAN HERALD
NEW YORK

CONTENTS

Introduction	7
The Gateway to the Holy Land	11
The Little Town of Bethlehem	21
Jerusalem the Joy of the Whole Earth	31
On the Way to Nazareth	43
Nazareth His Boyhood's Home	54
Beyond the Jordan	66
Around the Sea of Galilee	76
A Walk Beside the Lake	86
In the North Country	96
In and Around Ancient Shechem	108
From Jericho to Jerusalem	119

ILLUSTRATIONS

	Page
Joppa from the Sea	8
The Beach at Joppa	8
A Typical Street in Joppa	8
On the Nile, Egypt	8
The "Triumphal Road," Jerusalem	8
On the Mount of Olives	8
A Street in the Holy City	32
The "Street of Steps," Jerusalem	32
The Rocky Side of Golgotha	32
Gordon's Calvary (the "Garden Tomb")	32
Another View of the Via Dolorosa	33
The "Via Dolorosa" and the "Ecce Homo" Arch	33
In the Temple Grounds, Jerusalem	48
Church of the Holy Sepulchre	48
The "Old Wall," Jerusalem	49
Jerusalem, the Mosque of Omar, and Olivet in the Distance	56
An Archway in Jerusalem	56
Golgotha, the "Place of a Skull"	56
The Grotto of the Nativity	56
The "Garden Tomb"	56
The "Wailing Place" of the Jews	56
Types of Palestine Natives	56
Street Venders on the Joppa Road	56
Drivers and Donkey Boys	56
General View of Nazareth	56
At the "Fountain of the Virgin," Nazareth	57
Tiberias, from the Lake	64
Fishermen on the Sea of Galilee	65

Illustrations

	Page
THE ROAD TO BETHLEHEM	65
CANA OF GALILEE	80
GETHSEMANE AND MOUNT OF OLIVES, FROM THE TEMPLE	80
A MOHAMMEDAN MARKET PLACE	81
DAMASCUS, OLDEST CITY IN THE WORLD	88
THE MOSQUE OF OMAR, JERUSALEM	88
HOUSETOPS IN BETHLEHEM	88
GENERAL VIEW OF BETHLEHEM	88
AT "DAVID'S WELL," NEAR JERUSALEM	88
"CHURCH OF THE NATIVITY," BETHLEHEM	89
THE TOMB OF RACHEL	89
THE RIVER JORDAN	89
THE "MOUNT OF BEATITUDES"	89
A PALESTINE BEGGAR	89
NATIVE TYPES	89
THE VALLEY WHERE ELIJAH WAS FED BY RAVENS	89
PRAYER ON THE SAHARA DESERT	89
THE CITADEL OF CAIRO, EGYPT	104
SPHINX AND PYRAMID	104
THE EDGE OF THE DESERT	104
A ROW OF WONDERFUL PILLARS, LUXOR	105
AMID THE RUINS OF LUXOR	105
COLOSSI IN THE DESERT	105
A TEMPLE ENTRANCE, KARNAK	105
AMID KARNAK'S RUINED TEMPLES	105

FULL PAGE COLOR PLATES

THE GARDEN OF GETHSEMANE	Frontispiece
THE TRADITIONAL HOUSE OF SIMON THE TANNER, AT JOPPA	24
JERUSALEM, FROM THE MOUNT OF OLIVES	60
GENERAL VIEW OF BETHLEHEM	96

BY WAY OF INTRODUCTION

THERE is a little oblong strip on the map of the world that borders the eastern shore of the Mediterranean, to which more eyes turn with love and reverence than to any other part of this round earth, I might almost say to all other parts of the earth.

It is about the shape, and approximately the size of the state of New Hampshire, yet here have been enacted the Divine Tragedy, and a multitude of human tragedies.

For five millenniums conquering armies, with proudly waving banners, have marched across its blood-sodden soil, or have shrunk away from it decimated and defeated. The Kings of Chaldea and of Babylon, the Pharaos of Egypt, Joshua and David, the Generals of Israel, Alexander the Great and his generals, the Cæsars, the Crusaders, the Moslems, Napoleon and Napier, the greatest warriors of ancient and modern times, have sought to make it their own.

A thousand volumes would not tell minutely the history of this little state. But there was one event that took place there that overshadows all the history that preceded and succeeded it. A Babe was born, grew up, and died there, and though His short life spanned only a third of one of the 500 centuries of its history, it is because of His life and death that it is the holiest of holy lands to half the world.

I need not write the name of this wonderful land. My readers know it already. It is as familiar to them as their own native state. Many of them have longed to visit it, but circumstances have prevented, perhaps will always prevent, them from making their fondest dream a reality.

It is my desire in this volume to be eyes and ears and feet for them.

I have journeyed for them, gazed for them, listened for them. I have tried to imagine them with me, that we might see together the places of which we have all dreamed.

We will view together not only the holy spots which thousands of travellers, at the expense of thousands of dollars, travel thousands of miles to see, but we will occasionally stop to look at the people in their shops and cafés, in their homes, and at the workbench. We will listen to their weird cries as they sell their wares, we will catch, I hope, some inspiration from the magnificent scenery by sea and shore, and, above all, I trust our faith will be quickened and our view of spiritual things clarified, as we follow in the footsteps of our blessed Lord and His apostles, and of the prophets who foretold His coming.

I have called the book, "IN CHRIST'S OWN COUNTRY," because *our* journey has so far as possible followed *His* journeys, though of course not in minute detail. His years of active ministry were years of constant travel throughout Galilee, and even

JOPPA FROM THE SEA.

THE BEACH AT JOPPA.

A TYPICAL STREET IN JOPPA.

ON THE NILE, EGYPT.

On the Mount of Olives.

The "Triumphal Road," Jerusalem.

By Way of Introduction

to the coasts of Tyre and Sidon, and back and forth from Galilee to Jerusalem, sometimes on the east of the Jordan, though usually on the western side, and sometimes through Samaria, north as far as Mount Hermon, and west as far as the Mediterranean.

Thus in following Him we are able not only to see where He did His mighty works, and where He spoke His life-giving words, but we are able to visit the scenes made memorable by the Old Testament worthies as well as the New; scenes where kings and conquerors, and Crusaders fought their battles and built their empires, empires which, compared with the deathless kingdom of the Peasant of Nazareth, so soon crumbled to dust.

Indeed, if we omit Damascus from the list, the journeys of the Master take us to all the most interesting places in Palestine and Syria, so that in following Him through His Own Country we pass by few places in the Holy Land that are best worth seeing.

I send the book on its mission, conscious of its imperfections, as who would not be in dealing with such a subject, but hoping that the text and the abundant illustrations, taken on the spot especially for this volume, may make more real the land of the patriarchs and the prophets, of the psalmists and the apostles, and, above all, the land which, in a peculiar sense, was "His Own Country," who more and more, with every passing year, is becoming the Lord and Ruler of all.

Boston, June, 1914.   Francis E. Clark.

THE GATEWAY TO THE HOLY LAND

WITH what mingled feelings of awe, reverence and affection have a thousand times ten thousand of pilgrims, in all the centuries past, approached the gateways to the Holy Land! The Crusaders, nearly a millennium ago, with pæans of praise, over and over again turned the prows of their vessels hitherward, and in these latter days, following their example, though on a more peaceful errand bent, unnumbered multitudes of pilgrims, from remotest Russia, from busy Germany, from practical, unsentimental Great Britain, from all the Latin countries, and not a few from far-off America and Australia, every year crowd these shores.

Beyond these gateways lies the land that stirs their deepest sentiment and arouses their most profound adoration. Here is the country of Old Testament story and adventure, the land of which David sang, the country which the prophets loved so well that they dared denounce the follies of its people, the home of Abraham, and Isaac, and Jacob, the country where Peter and

James and John lived the humble life of Galilean fishers of fish, and afterwards became the "fishers of men," the land where Matthew collected taxes, and Luke healed the sick, where Paul gained a vision of the Master he had been so bitterly persecuting, and above all, and more than all put together, the land of Him who spake as never man spake, and Who here, for three and thirty years, went about doing good.

Nor must we forget that hither come also Mohammedan pilgrims; for next to Mecca and Medina, there is no such holy place to them as the rocky height in the midst of Jerusalem, where Solomon's Temple once stood, and which is now crowned by the beautiful Mosque of Omar.

But perhaps the emotions of no other race is so deeply stirred as those of the ancient people of God, when first they approach their fatherland. Though "scattered and peeled" and divided among the nations in the four quarters of the globe, this is still their home country, Jerusalem is still their capital city.

Thus we see that the three dominant races of the world—Christians, Jews, Mohammedans—comprising nearly half the inhabitants of our globe, turn their eyes hither with love and longing.

There are three chief gateways to Palestine today, Beyrout on the north, which though not in Palestine proper, is connected by rail with some of its most important sections; Haifa in the centre, under the shadow of Mount Carmel; and Jaffa, the old Joppa, in the south. Of the three Jaffa offers by far the most uncomfortable doorway to Palestine. With scarcely the semblance of a harbor, it lies on an open roadstead, which is often swept by turbulent winds that frequently render landing absolutely impossible. Jaffa only holds its own as a principal port for pilgrims because of its proximity to Jerusalem, the first and chief goal of most travellers in the Holy Land.

The dread of going ashore at Jaffa has doubtless kept many nervous souls from visiting the land of their desires, but the Gorgons at the Gate are after all not so dreadful as they are often pictured, for though an average of nearly three ships a day land their passengers or cargo at this port, few accidents are recorded. However, we are not allowed to forget the company of tourists who, a few years ago were pitched into these seething waves and drowned while the boatmen were holding them up for backshish and thus neglecting their oars.

But nowadays, if the landing is supposed to be seriously dangerous, the steamers plough on their way and land their passengers in the comparatively safe harbor of Haifa, about sixty miles further north.

At the best, however, the landing is a somewhat frightful one for timid mortals, for the sea is seldom very smooth. The strong boatman who has come for his fare grasps the passenger around the waist, hustles him down the slippery steps which hang on the ship's black side and into the waiting boat which is bobbing up and down, and thumping against the bottom of the steps. Then with the long sweeps he is carried over the intervening mile that separates him from the shore, sometimes finding himself in the depths of the trough of the wave, with nothing visible but the green waters of the Mediterranean on every side, and now hoisted to its crest with a wide panorama of sea and shore stretching before him, and with another wave bigger than the last apparently coming to engulf him.

The Hebrews called this port "Jaffa the Beautiful," and our first glimpse of Jaffa from the sea would seem to confirm the ancient title. Let us make the most of it, for as soon as we land on the slimy stones which serve for a pier, and climb the narrow, filthy streets that lead into the heart of the town, we shall revise our opinion and think that Jaffa must have sunk far from its high estate if it ever deserved its name.

However, we can excuse much in the way of filth and squalor for we find ourselves, as soon as we set foot on solid ground, to be in the land of romance, as well as of sacred history.

Even before we step ashore, as we come within the circle of ragged rocks, which protect us somewhat from the violence of the waves, we are reminded of the ancient myth of Andromeda, the daughter of Cepheus and Cassiopeia, who was herself the daughter of the wind god Æolus, for it is here, as we learned in our mythology, that Andromeda was chained to the rocks near which we are about to land until she was unchained by the gallant Perseus, who thus delivered her from the sea monster that was about to devour her.

At last our feet are upon the solid stone and mortar of the little quay. An overwhelming sense of the antiquity as well as of the exceeding interest of his surroundings strikes the tourist almost dumb as he stands for the first time on these shores. He may not be a Philistine, but he is actually in the Land of the Philistines, the long time bitter enemies of Israel. Here came the Carthaginians to found a colony on this Philistine shore. Here came the rafts of Hiram king of Tyre. "We will cut wood out of Lebanon," said the generous Hiram to Solomon the magnificent, "as much as thou shalt need, and we will bring it to thee in floats by sea to Joppa, and thou shalt carry it to Jerusalem." Again, in the days of Ezra, when the second temple was built "cedar trees were brought from Lebanon to the sea unto Joppa, according to the grant that they had of Cyrus, King of Persia."

Here too came that ill-fated mariner, Jonah, for we are told that he "went down to Joppa and found a ship going to Tarsus. So he paid the fare thereof, and went down into it, to go with them unto Tarshish from the presence of Jehovah."

If we should journey up the coast a hundred miles

further north we should find a beach of yellow sand between Sidon and Beyrout, where his disastrous voyage is said to have ended. Near by is a whitewashed Mohammedan tomb whose custodian tells us with all seriousness that Jonah is buried there, and to prove it he will even show us the wooden coffin of the rebellious prophet in the vault below.

But we must not linger longer on the shore. Dodging the porters with heavy trunks on their backs, the donkeys and the goats, and an occasional swaying camel with his heavy burden on either side, which often seems to fill the narrow roadway from curb to curb, we make our way over the rough cobblestones into the heart of the little city.

Before we lose the vividness of our first impressions of the strange sights which surround us we must record them in our notebooks, for after a few days or weeks in the Holy Land they will seem so natural and commonplace as to make little impression upon us.

The market square is always one of the most interesting spots to the traveller in a new land, and Jaffa's market place is no exception to the rule. Here have come the peasant women from the country with baskets of vegetables and fruit upon their heads; red tomatoes and yellow oranges; ripe green peppers, some of them turning to a brilliant crimson, match the reds and greens and yellows in the peasant's dress, and these bright colors somewhat relieve the poverty and squalor of which their rags and dirt tell us.

Some of them have eggs and chickens, and jars of sour milk, to sell, and if we reach the market place in the early part of the day, we shall see that many of the women have a queer bundle upon their backs as well as a heavy basket of vegetables upon their heads. Out from one end of this bundle peeps a little black head, and from the other a pair of baby's feet, for the mother must not only be a gardener and a saleswoman, but a nurse at the same time, since she cannot leave the baby at home.

There are men in the market place as well as women. They wear long blue cotton shirts reaching down to their feet, with a striped cloak of rough goats' hair over it, sandals on their feet, and different kinds of headgear, which proclaim their nationality, as distinctly as a top hat indicates an Englishman.

The Bedouin declares that he is from the free, wind-swept desert by the heavy cord of camel's hair that he wears around his crown. The red fez tells us that the man beneath it is a Mohammedan, or possibly a Syrian Christian, while the Jew is known by his little skullcap, beneath which dangle two cork-screw curls on either side.

The coffee-houses in the East are always places of interest and amusement to the traveller, and we shall find many in the vicinity of the bazaar, or market place of Jaffa. Here sit the men on low stools, or perhaps cross-legged on the floor, sipping cups of thick, black coffee, or smoking the bubbling narghileh, or waterpipe, and undoubtedly exchanging the latest Jaffa gossip or most savory scandal with their neighbors. The men have these cafés to themselves for the women are, for the most part, debarred from their sacred precincts.

But we have not time to linger long in the market place or café, for the train soon starts for Jerusalem, and there are several places that we must see before we take our seats therein. We must climb the Russian church-tower and get a complete view of Jaffa. The higher we get the less mean and tawdry does the city look. In the north we can see the shadowy outlines of Mt. Carmel. To the east we can see far off on the Plain of Sharon, and if it is springtime it is a fair and lovely sight indeed, dotted with orange groves and olive orchards and green with waving grain. As we approach nearer we shall see the wonderfully variegated anenomes, which make the whole land bright and gay, with their many-hued brilliance. These, perhaps, were the roses of Sharon, celebrated in song and story.

If we have lately read the book of Acts, we are not likely to forget that Peter "abode many days in Joppa, with one Simon a tanner." It is not difficult to find the alleged house of Simon the tanner today, though there are two claimants for the honor. A Latin hospice covers the site which is most commonly pointed out to the traveller, though a little mosque at some distance to the south of the hospice also has its stout adherents as the very place where Peter had that wonderful vision when he went up on the housetop to pray. This vision of the sheet let down from heaven, containing "all manner of four-footed beasts and creeping things of the earth, and birds of the air," so broadened Peter's sympathies that he could no longer call anything "common or unclean," and made him ready to receive the messengers of Cornelius, the captain of the Italian cohort, who had come from Cesarea at the command of his master to invite Peter to visit him.

The story of that scene in Joppa is worth reading over and over again, for it was one of the crises in the life of Peter, and one of the turning points in the history of the Church. What matters it if we do not know the exact spot where the tanner lived! We know that somewhere in this ancient town, which we saw from end to end from the church tower, this great event occurred, and, in imagination at least, we can see the Italian soldiers of Cornelius galloping down the long road from Cesarea on the north, the unconscious messengers of God from the Gentile world.

Nor must we forget to visit the supposed site of the home and rock tomb of Tabitha (Dorcas) which we shall find in the Russian settlement, only a few minutes' walk from the market place in the centre of the town. She must have been a beautiful woman if her name, which signifies a gazelle, means anything. At least she was beautiful in spirit and in character, and noted for her alms deeds, and for "the coats and garments which she made and gave to the poor." We remember the miracle which Peter wrought when he raised her from the dead, with the simple words spoken in the Master's name and power, "Tabitha, arise!"

The miracles that Dorcas' example and memory have wrought since are scarcely less wonderful than that which Peter wrought. How many Christian women she has inspired to like alms deeds! How many sewing circles and mission bands have been called after her name, and what a multitude of coats and garments have been the generous product of these Dorcas societies throughout the world!

As we leave Jaffa for the heart of Palestine, let us call to mind the noble, Christian, democratic sentiment embodied in Peter's words to the Centurion of Cesarea, after he had learned his great lesson on the Jaffa housetop. "Of a truth I perceive that God is no respecter of persons, but, in every nation he that feareth Him and worketh righteousness is acceptable to Him."

THE LITTLE TOWN OF BETHLEHEM

HAD we time to linger longer in Jaffa we would learn more of the Christian work which is now carried on there; and would see the hospitals and schools of the Latin and Greek churches, and especially the English Protestant mission house and hospital.

In the "Jerusalem Hotel," where we take our lunch before starting on our four hours' railway ride, we are interested to see that the rooms are named for Bible characters. There is a "Tabitha Room," and a "Peter Room," and other Bible rooms. Could we spend a night in this hotel, we would ask to be assigned to the "Peter Room," hoping for a glorious vision such as he saw in ancient Joppa. But the guard is calling out "All aboard for Jerusalem," and we must take our places in one of the compartments of the little train that soon speeds over the Plain of Sharon, first winding its way through the glorious orange groves, for which Jaffa is famous in all the world, for there are no other oranges like the golden fruit of Jaffa.

A dozen miles out of the city we come to Lydda. Here Peter was living when he was called to Joppa to the bedside of Tabitha. Here he healed the palzied Æneas, who had been bed-ridden for eight years. "Jesus Christ healeth thee," Peter had said to him; "arise and make thy bed!"

Then the train hurries on to Ramleh, thought by some to have been the home of Joseph of Arimathea. Every mile of this wonderful journey is crowded with memories of Bible scenes. There is Ekron, of which we are told in the book of Joshua, which was one of the five principal cities of Palistia, and which now contains a Jewish colony founded by the great house of Rothschild. Near by is Gezer which we are told in the first book of Kings was captured by Pharaoh king of Egypt, who "burnt it with fire and slew the Canaanites that dwelt in the city, and gave it for a portion to his daughter, Solomon's wife." This ancient city has been explored by the Palestine Exploration Society, and the Egyptian seals and rings in the midst of the relics of the Canaanites confirm the Bible story concerning Solomon's father-in-law.

After passing through the fertile plain of Sharon, our engine begins to puff laboriously, and the road winds along the edge of cavernous defiles with towering mountains of bare rock looming up on either side. Mightily impressive in their stern grandeur are these mountains that lie round about Jerusalem on her western side, but so stript of every sign of vegetation, that they leave upon the mind the impression of gloomy sterility which many other parts of Palestine confirm.

In Bible times, however, it was "a land flowing with milk and honey." It supported an enormous population, many times larger than at present. We can only account for the modern barren and denuded Palestine by the folly of the inhabitants in cutting down the trees, and rendering it as it is to-day, largely a desolate, treeless land. Even in the reign of Solomon we are told this destruction had begun. "In the times of the Assyrian, and after the fall of Jerusalem, the population of Palestine was largely deported, irrigation was suspended, the rains, falling on unprotected slopes, washed the soil down into the valleys, and the hills became bare as to-day."

May the people of America learn the lesson which Palestine teaches, and by preserving her forests, or restoring them where they have been destroyed, escape the fate which has rendered so much of the Holy Land barren and deserted.

About half way between Jaffa and Jerusalem we come into Samson's country, and we see a deep grotto far up on the mountain side which is called Samson's Cavern. It was in this region that many of his curious adventures are located. Here he caught the three hundred foxes or jackals, and with fire-brands tied to their tails, according to the story in Judges, "let them go into the standing grain of the Philistines and burnt up both the shocks and the standing grain, and also the olive yards." Samson has been well called the humorist of the Old Testament, and his story, incredible as it appears to many modern Biblical critics, gives us a rare glimpse of the people of those ancient days, who dwelt in the country through which we are now travelling, incongruous as it seems, on a modern railway line, carried over these granite mountainous regions by a puffing, snorting, American locomotive.

Up, up we climb, some thousands of feet above the sea level until at last the train stops and the guard cries out "Jerusalem!"

We cannot see the city from the railway station, which is nearly a mile from the Jaffa Gate. To-day we will not enter within its walls, since, so far as possible, we desire to visit our Lord's country in the order of the events of His life upon earth. So we will go first of all to the place where He was born.

We will therefore take one of the rickety cabs which await us at the railway station, and unlike most travellers, instead of entering Jerusalem at this time, will take the southern road, which leads to Bethlehem, some six miles away. We are glad to see from the posters on the wall that there is a "Jerusalem Society for the Prevention of Cruelty to Animals" for if ever such a society is needed anywhere, it is in Palestine to-day, and we hope our driver will be merciful to his raw-boned beast.

THE TRADITIONAL HOUSE OF SIMON THE TANNER, AT JOPPA.

The Little Town of Bethlehem

It is but a short ride, indeed, filling but little more than an hour's time, but what uncounted ages of history, what pathetic and sacred scenes, what memories of war and bloodshed, could this ancient highway tell us, if we could read its whole story! The traditions, however difficult it may be to believe them in minute particulars, are still in a large and general way accurate, since we know that all these great events occurred, and occurred in this immediate vicinity.

We have barely started on our drive before we see on the left the "Hill of Evil Counsel," where it is said that the villa of Caiaphas once stood, where he consulted with the hostile Jews concerning the death of Jesus. A mile or two further on is the "Well of the Magi," where the Star of Bethlehem is said to have shone upon them once more, and where we are told that Mary rested on her way to Jerusalem. The Ophthalmic Hospital of the Knights of St. John, the Nunnery and Monastery and the other modern buildings which we see soon after leaving the railway station, rather interfere with the memories of the past, and in order to get back to the ancient days which make this little country sacred and famous we have to clear away, in imagination, many modern innovations.

The most interesting, as well as the most authentic site on the Bethlehem road is the Tomb of Rachel. It is true that the present tomb is comparatively modern, and has probably been rebuilt many a time within the last thousand years, but an almost unbroken tradition confirms the story which we read in Genesis, and alluded to in First Samuel and Jeremiah, that here was the very spot where Rachel died and was buried "in the way to Ephrath, the same is Bethlehem. And Jacob set up a pillar upon her grave."

From the time of Christ, no other spot has been suggested as Rachel's burying place, and Christians, Jews and Mohammedans alike visit it in reverent faith, and have inscribed their names upon its walls, in irreverent desire for a species of immortality, and the hope of linking their names with that of the mother of patriarchs. To-day the tomb is not inspiring from an architectural standpoint, but is like a hundred other Mohammedan welis, or tombs, which we shall see in Palestine.

Even before we reach Rachel's tomb our Lord's birthplace breaks upon our eager gaze, lying upon two ridges of chalky formation high above the valley through which we approach it. It is no longer "least among the cities of Judah," but almost the greatest of all towns to the Christian heart, the very greatest of all perhaps, if we except the city where He was crucified Who was born in Bethlehem. Its name Beth Lehem, means "Place of Bread." It has indeed been the place of the bread of life for many spiritually hungry souls.

We rejoice to note that all the region round about is, for Palestine, unusually fertile and productive. The terraces have been maintained by the retaining walls of heavy cut stone, and filled with the fertile soil from the valley below. Olive orchards and vineyards surround the city, and our first impression, especially as we look at it from a distance, is that it is a fit place indeed for the Saviour's birth. A multitude of emotions and memories surge through our hearts as we approach the city. There are the fields where David watched his flocks, and gazed up into the starry skies. The memory of those days and nights perhaps gave birth to the Shepherd Psalm and to that Psalm of the Starry Heavens, which tells of the "moon and the stars which thou didst ordain."

A walk of a few minutes from the roadside, just before we reach the city, brings us to *David's Well,* from which the Three Mighty Men brought in the water for which he longed, and which he would not drink, but "poured it out before the Lord." Our guidebook however detracts from the poetic memories of the well when it tells us that the "water is unwholesome."

Perhaps on the very fields where David kept his flock, or at least very near by, were the broad acres of Boaz where Ruth, David's grandmother, gleaned, after the reapers, and where the scene of the beautiful idyl of the book of Ruth is laid.

The evidences of cultivation and fertility indicate to us what the whole of Palestine, now so barren and dreary in many parts, once was.

A steep climb brings us to the gate of the city, and we enter its narrow streets with high and gloomy buildings of cut stone on either side. Our last impressions of Bethlehem, shall be of the place of the Nativity, that these impressions may not be dissipated by contact with meaner things. So we will first visit one or two of the large curio shops, to which persistent and insistent guides are constantly trying to direct our footsteps.

Here we shall find many beautiful things wrought in mother-of-pearl, in olive wood, in mosaics of different kinds, for Bethlehem is the centre for the manufacture of mother-of-pearl ornaments in all the world. Crucifixes and crosses, stars of Bethlehem, and beautifully inlaid boxes and necklaces of pearl, are piled by the thousand on the shelves of the merchants, and are exported from Bethlehem to the ends of the earth, all of them retaining something of the odor of sanctity in the nostrils of the pilgrims, because of the place wherein they are manufactured.

These trinkets, however, cannot long keep us away from the centre of attraction, the spot where Christ the Lord was born. We can comfort ourselves, too, with the reflection, as we approach this sacred shrine, that the traditions which assign this as His birthplace, are more trustworthy than almost any others connected with his life or death. Hundreds of years before Helena erected the church over his birthplace, and only a few years after the death of the apostle John, Justin Martyr assigned the manger cradle to "a certain cave close to the village of Bethlehem" and this cave was undoubtedly the grotto which is now called the Chapel of the Nativity.

Other church fathers who were in a position to know the truth in the early years of our era, confirm the genuineness of this site, and St. Jerome so thoroughly believed in it that he made his own home for many years in a grotto near by, and here gave us that most important translation of the Bible, the Latin Vulgate.

The church itself is a noble and massive building with a vast central aisle and two wide side aisles separated from the centre by two rows of massive columns, each one a single stone, twenty feet high and more than two feet in diameter. The roof of the church was originally made of the cedars of Lebanon, but English oak sent to Bethlehem in the reign of Edward IV. now covers the sacred edifice. Here Baldwin was crowned king of Jerusalem more than 800 years ago, on a Christmas day, and here myriads of pilgrims have turned their willing feet that they might gaze upon the spot where their Lord was born.

All other events connected with this famous church pale into insignificance in comparison with the one supreme event in the story of redemption.

With reverent feet and slow we approach the Chapel of the Nativity, at the east end of the church.

Its floor is of marble and the walls of the grotto are also chiefly marble, covered with draperies wrought with silk and gold. At the eastern end of the chapel is the spot to which all feet are irresistibly drawn. Here, in the marble floor, we see a silver star imbedded in the stone. Above it sixteen silver lamps are hung, which are never allowed to grow dim, and around the Star is the Latin inscription *"Hic de Virgine Maria Jesus Christus natus est."* It has been finely said, "Whatever we may think of the locality itself, that silver star in Bethlehem commemorates the greatest event in the long history of time. Here love became incarnate that love might suffer and redeem."

With such thoughts and such emotions stirring our deepest souls let us quietly and reverently depart from the birthplace of our Lord.

JERUSALEM THE JOY OF THE WHOLE EARTH

"If I forget thee, O Jerusalem, let my right hand forget her cunning."

OUR Lord was but a month old when, in accordance with the Jewish custom, his beautiful mother carried Him in her arms from humble Bethlehem to glorious Jerusalem for the presentation and purification in the temple.

In following Him thither we come to the city which, of all others in the world, is dear to Jew and Christian alike, while the Mohammedan also turns thither his willing feet in a holy pilgrimage. Hundreds of millions of Christians, in a hundred languages, sing,

> "O Mother dear, Jerusalem,
> Name ever dear to me;
> When shall my sorrows have an end,
> Thy joys when shall I see?"

But a small fraction of these millions ever see Jerusalem, the earthly, except with the eye of faith, and doubtless many of them, if they saw it only with the eye of sense and flesh would be woefully disappointed in the mean, squalid and dirty city which has succeeded the glorious metropolis of the time of Christ.

It is a historic fact that in all the long fourteen hundred years that it existed before the time of Christ, and the nearly two thousand years that have passed over its desolation since His time, it was never so proud and regal a city as, when in His mother's arms, our Lord entered it for the first time.

It is true that David made it his fortified home, and Solomon had embellished it with the riches of many lands, and the spoil of many victories. Hezekiah had enlarged its borders, giving it a fine water supply, and had dug many cisterns. But under King Herod the Edomite, assisted by the Romans, only a generation before the beginning of our era, Jerusalem had blossomed out afresh, after being destroyed and rebuilt over and over again by Egyptians, and Babylonians, and Greeks and Syrians. At this period, we are told, "Jerusalem with its numerous palaces and handsome edifices, the sumptuous temple with its colonnades, and the lofty city walls with their bastions, must have presented a very splendid appearance."

Josephus is often quoted as recording that at about this period 270,000 Paschal lambs were sacrificed at the great yearly feast of the Passover, which would indicate that there were more than two and a half millions

A STREET IN THE HOLY CITY.

THE "STREET OF STEPS," JERUSALEM.

THE ROCKY SIDE OF GOLGOTHA.

GORDON'S CALVARY (THE "GARDEN TOMB.")

The "Via Dolorosa" and the "Ecce Homo" Arch.

Another View of the Via Dolorosa.

of people in the city at this time. Josephus, however, must often be taken with a grain of salt, for it is known that he frequently liked to draw a long bow, and it is very difficult to believe, as we look at the shrunken little city, which seems to be crowded to the utmost with its 75,000 modern inhabitants, that more than thirty times that number could ever have found accommodations within its walls, or even in the immediate vicinity.

So far as we know our Master visited the capital of his country some seven or eight times in the course of His short life, and perhaps oftener if with His family He frequently attended the yearly Passover feast. Here He taught the doctors in the temple, a dozen years after Mary carried Him thither in her arms. Here He cast out the money changers, who were making his "Father's house a house of thieves." Here He rode in meek triumph on His one day of earthly acclaim, when the people cast their garments before Him and cried, "Hosanna!" Here, too, was enacted the tragedy of the Cross, and the final victory of the empty tomb.

When we consider these events, the mightiest in human history, Jerusalem seems no longer squalid and sordid, but is glorified by holy memories, and by suggestions of the new Jerusalem, of which the ancient city, to the Christian heart, has ever been the type.

"The value of these holy sites," it has been well said, "lie mainly in the heart which feels and the eyes which see. The most doubtful of them is still consecrated by the prayers, the tears, the painful pilgrimages of well nigh two thousand years." We may also say that the city is consecrated by the blood of its defenders and its assailants alike, for, since the time of our Lord, Jews and Christians, the ancient families of Jerusalem, and Crusaders from the far west have poured out their blood like water, in their efforts to retain or gain control of the holy city.

The Romans, the Persians, the Byzantine emperors from Constantinople, the Egyptians, the Turks, and the Crusaders have succeeded each other for a longer or shorter time, as rulers of the coveted city, but for almost four hundred years now, it has been in the practically undisturbed possession of the Moslems.

Let us visit first the spot to which the infant Jesus was carried when four weeks old, in the arms of His loving mother. Coming from Bethlehem, He probably entered Jerusalem by the Jaffa Gate as we do to-day. The gray walls which rear themselves on every side as we approach the city have been built and rebuilt many times since the days of Christ, and many times more since David made Jerusalem his fortress, but doubtless some of the ancient material enters into these modern walls, and some of the foundation stones date back to Christ's own day.

On the right, as we enter the Jaffa Gate, is the so-called Tower of David, grim and massive, and worthy of its name, even if David never looked upon it. On the other side is a clock tower of graceful proportions, rising from the wall of the city. It records Turkish time, a decidedly different set of hours from those recorded by clocks in Christian lands. According to the Turkish reckoning the sun always sets at twelve o'clock, summer and winter. One hour after sunset is one o'clock, two hours two o'clock, and so on, until the twenty-four hours of the day have rolled around, and twelve o'clock and sunset have come once more.

David Street is the first one we enter, as we pass through the Jaffa Gate, and we notice that though there are men and women and boys and girls, and camels and donkeys, and a few horses, there are no wheeled vehicles after we penetrate a little ways beyond the gate. A carriage could not go far in Jerusalem, for many of the streets seem more like tunnels than open thoroughfares. Many of them are a series of steps of massive stone, while others are so narrow that a loaded camel has almost as much difficulty in crowding his way through as a man who trusts in riches would have in entering the streets of the new Jerusalem.

The "Grand New Hotel" which is neither new nor grand, stands on the left just within the gate, and beyond this are two great shops for the sale of pictures, curios and antiquities, whose proprietors are very eager to entice one within their doors. In the one kept by the people of the "American Colony," a communistic group of colonists whose first members came here in order that they might rise with Christ from Jerusalem itself on the Resurrection day, one may be sure of obtaining fair treatment, as well as a hearty welcome. Sometimes they even advertise "Fresh Doughnuts and Squash Pies" to beguile the willing American tourist, and to remind him of the home land.

Soon after passing these stores David Street leads down a somewhat steep descent, lined on either side with little shops and stalls, where dry goods and groceries, vegetables, and wine and oil are dispensed in minute quantities for exceedingly small sums of money. Egg plants and radishes, carrots and potatoes, grapes, dates, oranges, melons, oil and olives, are forced upon our attention, for the little shops are all open in front, and one often has to make a detour in order to get by the vociferous vendor who calls out in raucous tones and poetical language the wares that he has to sell.

After a little David Street crosses Christian Street, which is also a narrow lane lined with shops of every kind, and later still the Via Dolorosa ("The Sorrowful Way"), which is supposed to follow the course of the pathetic journey of the Master from the house of Caiaphas to Golgotha.

But we are on our way first, not to the place of the cross, but to the site of the temple where the infant Jesus was presented by His parents.

Long, long ago, only a few decades after our

Saviour's death, that temple was destroyed, and "not one stone left upon another," in the awful and irremediable ruin which followed the siege of Titus, and now for many centuries a beautiful Turkish temple has covered the site of the glorious temple of the Jews.

In order to visit it we must obtain permission from our American consul, who arranges with the Turkish governor to send a gorgeously arrayed kavass to conduct us thither. He is covered with enough gold lace and braid and supplied with sufficient daggers and pistols to make himself duly impressive. But with all his gorgeousness he is not above accepting a few paras for his services. He leads us through various narrow streets to a great, flat enclosure surrounded by walls called the Haram-esh-Sherif. This is none other than the site of the magnificent temple of Solomon and the more glorious sanctuary built by Herod.

From the time of David it has been a sacred place. We may even go back further in the history of the world, for the "Dome of the Rock" is thought to be the spot where Abraham was about to sacrifice Isaac, when God rewarded his faith by sparing his son and giving him the promise of unnumbered descendants.

By far the most interesting object now in this sacred enclosure is the Moslem *Kubbet es-Sakhra,* or "Dome of the Rock." This building is usually called, though erroneously, the Mosque of Omar. It is deservedly one of the most noted buildings in the world. While not comparing for beauty or grandeur with the Taj Mahal in Agra, for instance, or even with some of the great cathedrals of Europe, it has a glory and an interest all its own. It is in the form of an octagon, each of the eight sides being more than 66 feet in length. The lower part is covered with marble, while above, giving a beautiful sheen to the whole structure, are porcelain tiles of a bluish tinge. Verses from the Koran are inscribed around the building on every side. Many of these verses, while giving honor to Jesus Christ, directly deny the Trinity, like the following:

"The Messiah Jesus is only the Son of Mary, the Ambassador of God, and His Word which He deposited in Mary. Believe then in God and His Ambassador, and do not maintain there are three."

Entering within this marvelous building we find a beautiful wrought-iron screen surrounding the rock itself, which, however, one can easily see through the interstices. The building contains any number of relics and of superstitious marvels connected with the life of the false prophet; hairs from Mohammed's beard, banners of Mohammed and Omar, ancient copies of the Koran, etc. In a rock slab set in the floor, a slab which is said to have been the cover of Solomon's tomb, were driven by Mohammed himself nineteen golden nails. Whenever an epoch ends a nail falls out, and when all are gone then comes the end of the world. We are solemnly told that the devil, desiring to hasten the end of the world, and claim mankind in its wickedness for his own, slyly drew out all of the nails but three and a half, when, luckily, the angel Gabriel discovered what he was about, and stopped his nefarious plans, so that now there are only three and a half nails left in the slab.

I cannot hope to tell all the foolish traditions that have gathered about this historic site; about the fingerprints of Gabriel on the stone, or the footprint of Mohammed in the solid rock, from which he rose to heaven on the back of El-Burak, his wonderful horse; how he hit his head against the ceiling and left a deep impression there, while an angel held down the rock and prevented its following him to the skies.

Thickly as the historical places, more dear to the Christian heart, are overlaid with traditions, we may be thankful that none are so silly and absurd as those with which we are regaled at the Dome of the Rock.

However brief our visit to Jerusalem, there is one more spot which we must not fail to see, the Church of the Holy Sepulchre. The Wailing Place of the Jews, though it tells of the bitter sorrows of a scattered and dispersed, but wonderfully virile, people, has little about it to stimulate the Christian's heart, but the Church of the Holy Sepulchre is for him the Holy of Holies.

Let us not look with too critical an eye for the exact verification of these sacred places. The attitude of some people on approaching them is well characterized by a writer in the London Times, who said, "We have been taught by a long series of skeptical inquiries to take it almost for granted that if, according to an ancient tradition a famous event happened in a particular spot, it must really have happened somewhere else, unless, indeed, it never happened at all."

But traditions have their weight, and the overwhelming evidence of tradition places the crucifixion of our Lord at least very near the spot which is now covered by the Church of the Holy Sepulchre. It is true that for a time, eminent scholars were inclined to suppose that a place outside the modern walls, on a hill now covered by Moslem graves, was the true Golgotha, but the most recent research seems to veer back to the ancient site.

However that may be, we will sadly and thoughtfully walk down the Sorrowful Way, from the Turkish barracks which stand on the spot of the ancient Prætorium, where Jesus was tried. Here is the first Station of the Cross, and we follow these stations one after another, down the Via Dolorosa, under the Ecce Homo Arch, where tradition says Pilate presented his divine prisoner to the Jews, saying "Behold the Man," on and on, under the vaulted arches, past one station after another, until we come to the fourteenth and last station, which is beside the Holy Sepulchre itself.

The outside of the church is not particularly impressive, though the great dome with the golden cross surmounting it, can be seen from many parts of the city. The inside, too, is at first disappointing, largely because of a multitude of ornaments, which seem to detract from the sacredness of the place, so full do they fill the eyes with gold and silver and tinsel, lamps and candlesticks, and bric-a-brac of all kinds which devout pilgrims have brought from the ends of the earth to the holy church.

We must try, however, to forget these extraneous things, and remember that here, or very near here, our dear Lord was crucified, "who died to save us all."

Soon after entering we come to the "Stone of Unction," on which the body of Jesus is reputed to have been laid out for His burial. A few steps more bring us under the great dome of the church, which rests upon eighteen stone pillars. Under the very centre of the dome is the holy sepulchre itself, in a little chapel of marble all its own. It is but a tiny chapel some six feet square, but the ceiling is studded with golden lamps which belong to the four different sects, the Greek Catholic, the Latin Catholic, the Armenian and the Copt. Here, according to the belief of the great majority of Christians, lay the body of our Lord during the three eventful days when death claimed Him for its own.

Coming out of the chapel of the Holy Sepulchre we find in another part of the church numerous chapels, like the Chapel of the Prison of Christ where He was confined with the two thieves before the crucifixion.

The Chapel of the Parting of the Raiment, the Chapel of the Crown of Thorns, the Chapel of the Derision, each one of which marks a spot supposed to be connected with the trial and death of our Lord, until at last we come to the Chapel of the Raising of the Cross. In this chapel a hole is shown in the rock lined with silver, where our Lord's cross is supposed to have been inserted, while on either side, five feet distant, are the holes for the crosses of the two thieves, the Penitent Thief on the right or south side, and the Impenitent Thief on the north.

There are many other chapels and holy sites, but I will not confuse my readers by trying to locate them. Some of them, like the Tomb of Adam, and the hole that leads to the centre of the earth, are almost too grotesque to be spoken of in this connection.

Whatever scholars may finally decide is the true site of our Lord's cross and tomb, I must say that it is more satisfactory to leave the tawdry church and go outside the city walls to the so-called "Gordon Tomb," and meditate in the free air, and under the blue Judean sky, on the tremendous truth that somewhere on this mountain-top city our Lord was crucified and buried, and from it rose again to die no more, but to live forever that we might live.

ON THE WAY TO NAZARETH

AFTER the presentation in the temple we may suppose that Joseph and Mary took the infant Jesus back to their temporary home in Bethlehem, but the dreadful news soon reached their ears that the wicked Herod, the child-murderer, would "seek the young Child to destroy Him." So with their few belongings, and their precious first-born Son, they set out for Egypt, some eighty or a hundred miles distant. We know little about this episode in our Lord's life, but ever busy tradition points out to travellers near Cairo, the Virgin's Tree, under which Mary rested with the Infant Jesus, while artists have allowed their imagination free play, and have shown us the Infant Jesus and His parents resting under the shadow of the Pyramids, and even in the arms of the Sphinx itself.

We will not however take any liberties with Scripture narratives, but return with the Holy Family, after two years, to their own country, when the angel had told them that *"they are dead which sought the young Child's life."*

However, Joseph distrusted the bad blood of the

Herod family, and when he learned that Archelaus "did reign over Judea in the room of his father, Herod, he was afraid to go thither, . . . and turned aside into the parts of Galilee; and he came and dwelt in a city called Nazareth."

We do not know the exact route which the Holy Family took on their long, slow journey from Egypt to northern Palestine, but it is altogether probable that in order to avoid dangerous Judea they would follow the seashore route through the ancient country of the Philistines, through Jaffa, Cesarea, to the region of Mount Carmel, when they would turn directly east to the little hill-encircled village of Nazareth.

We will follow this route, for it takes us through a most interesting stretch of country, over almost the whole of Palestine-on-the-Sea, and through some places which we must not fail to visit if we will become acquainted with Palestine as it was in the time of Christ and as it is to-day.

Geographers divide Palestine into four longitudinal sections. The Lebanon and Anti-Lebanon mountains, which in the north rise to a height of 10,000 feet in snowy Hermon, gradually diminish in size as we go south toward Egypt, and end near Sinai in the desert. East of this central range lies the deep valley of the Jordan with the Lake of Galilee toward the north and the Dead Sea in the south. This is indeed one of the most wonderful valleys in the world. Were there no sacred associations connected with it, still it would interest geographers and tourists from all lands, for it is a valley that seems to lead one into the very bowels of the earth. Even at the Sea of Galilee we find ourselves 680 feet below the level of the sea.

Down, down the Jordan plunges through its rugged and frightful defiles 610 feet more before it empties itself into the Dead Sea, where the traveller is more than a quarter of a mile lower than the waves of the Mediterranean. On the east side of the Jordan valley is another smaller range of mountains, while on the western side of the central range is the maritime plain, sometimes narrowed to a mere ribbon of land, and sometimes widening into broad and fertile prairies, like the Plain of Sharon, and the country of the Philistines, to the south of this plain.

Such are the great features of Palestinian geography. A fertile seashore tract, a range of bold, impressive mountains, a long, deep gorge with a historic river flowing through it, and another range of smaller hills on the other side.

Before we have seen all the sacred places of Palestine we shall take several different routes, sometimes over the mountains, sometimes through the valley, but to-day we will follow the course of the Infant Jesus on His first journey to His boyhood home in Nazareth.

It is most likely that this road led through ancient Joppa, which we have already seen, when we first landed in Palestine, since this city, for many generations before the time of Christ, had been on the highway from Egypt to the north.

The next place of interest which we reach on this journey, retains to-day scarcely the shadow of a shade of its ancient glory. This is Cesarea. So abandoned is this place to-day that much of the year it is inaccessible, at least for carriages. Only a few ruins and a few filthy stone huts tell of the splendid city which existed here in the time of Christ. It even surpassed Jerusalem in political importance. Here was an enormous theatre that accommodated 20,000 spectators, and another theatre where gladiators fought, and which on occasion could be filled with sea water to provide for nautical sports, and mimic naval contests.

We are especially interested in Cesarea, because here the apostle Paul spent two long years in its dreary prison, chained probably day and night to a Roman soldier, though he was allowed some privileges, and the companionship of friends and fellow Christians. Here, under the corrupt Felix, and the more just and generous Festus he lived, and took occasion to preach the glad tidings of the new faith not only to the soldiers of many lands, which formed the Roman garrison, but to people of the highest authority, like Felix, and Festus, and Agrippa and Bernice his queen. Here he appealed to Cæsar, and demanded a trial at Rome, and from this place he set forth on his adventurous voyage, reaching at last, after a thrilling shipwreck and many adventures, the Eternal City.

Here, too, came Peter, at an earlier date, when summoned by Cornelius, the centurion, who commanded the Italian troops of Cesarea. We have already seen his soldiers galloping to Joppa, and have seen how willingly Peter obeyed the divine command, in hurrying to Cesarea, where he made one of the first Gentile converts to Jesus Christ. Here the Holy Spirit fell "on all them that heard the word," and here they were baptized in the name of Jesus Christ.

Cesarea was a modern town in the time of Christ, newer even than some of our great American cities, for it had the power and influence of Rome quickly to build it up to its magnificent proportions. But its decline was as rapid as its rise to power, and probably no great city of antiquity within the borders of Palestine is now such an utter wreck and ruin. The wild waves of the Mediterranean dash over the enormous blocks of granite which can still be seen beneath the water, and day and night sing the requiem of the ancient glories and the present decay of this great metropolis.

It is interesting to remember that the little family in its northward journey probably saw many of the same familiar sights that we see to-day. The common phrase "the unchanging East" has a large measure of truth in it. In spite of the few railways and carriage roads which make Palestine more easy of exploration to-day, the customs of the people and their costumes have doubtless changed but little during these three thousand years.

For instance, we see on this journey many Bedouins, or desert-dwellers, looking very much as the child Jesus must have seen them. Many of them are kindly men, and we can imagine that they would stop to gaze at the humble little caravan, and mayhap they took the little One in their arms, and perhaps gave him a ride on one of their fine horses, while the father and mother, with the patient ass, trudged on more slowly behind. "Well may these desert-dwellers be proud," says one, "for these descendants from Abraham's son, Ishmael, unlike the Jews, the poor captive descendants from his other son Isaac, have never once been conquered and subjugated by another nation, but have enjoyed unbroken freedom ever since, some 4,000 years ago, they began their national life." We know these men to-day, as they were doubtless known then, chiefly by their peculiar headdress, with the camel's hair rope around their heads.

There were the fellaheen, too, or the peasants, whom we see in such large numbers to-day. Jesus belonged to this peasant class, and the word Fellaheen, by which they were known, means "cultivator" or "ploughman." They wear to-day, as in the olden days doubtless, a long white tunic for the under garment, and often for their only garment. It is wide and full and reaches to the

IN THE TEMPLE GROUNDS, JERUSALEM.

CHURCH OF THE HOLY SEPULCHRE.

THE "OLD WALL," JERUSALEM.

ankles, and is fastened around the waist by a leather or worsted girdle. When they have a journey to make, or hard work to do, they "gird up their loins" by taking up the front of their tunic and tucking it into the girdle, leaving their legs naked and free for walking or working. Over this they often wear a striped brown and white or brown and blue camel's hair cloak, the stripes of which always run up and down. This cloak is quite water-proof, and like the burnous of the Arabs and the blanket of the South American shepherds, which has a hole in the middle through which they put their heads, serves almost the purpose of a tent in cold and rainy weather.

Sometimes at night the Holy Family would doubtless sleep in one of the numerous khans which were found on every important highway, and which we frequently find even in the present decadent condition of Palestine. These are usually built of stone. Entering a low door, we find ourselves in a spacious courtyard, where donkeys and camels and horses and their drivers, with wagons and bales of goods, are all mingled in apparent confusion. Around the sides of the khan are little cubicles where one may sleep, and sometimes there is a second story with a gallery over the lower rooms. For the most part they are dirty and dismal caravansaries and lodging only is usually furnished, though sometimes one can get a cup of black coffee, or a few oranges.

Possibly, however, Joseph had a tent of camel's hair, and every night he may have pitched it in some convenient place, just as we find them pitched to-day. The Arabs call this tent "a House of Hair." The cloth is woven by the women into strips about twenty-seven inches wide, and is said to absorb the rays of the sun so as to make the tent in hot weather much cooler than the tents of white canvas, as well as far more impervious to the rain.

Thus the little family would journey on day after day, until at last they see a great cliff, rising up almost sheer from the sea, and they know that they are approaching famous Mount Carmel. In all Palestine I have seen few more striking scenes or spots more full of historic interest than this same noble hill. One can see it from afar, as he approaches, either from the sea or from the land. From Nazareth it shows us where the Great Sea lies, and hour after hour, as we journey on any of the roads which leads to the north of Palestine, this historic mountain is ever in view.

It rises nearly 2,000 feet above the sea which laves its base. It does not rise to a single peak like many mountains, but rather ascends gently towards a long, wide plateau, reminding one remotely of Table Mountain in South Africa. It stretches along the shore and inland for about twelve miles, and because of the heavy dew which falls upon it is green and fresh through a large portion of the year, a blessed sight in

Palestine for tired eyes that in the hot season have looked only on the bare, brown hills. Isaiah speaks of it as "the excellency of Carmel," and Solomon in his Song of Songs says of the prince's daughter, "Thy head upon thee is like Carmel."

The view from the top of Carmel is superb indeed. As one stands upon the long level top, he can see the "great and wide sea" on one side, ruined Cesarea to the south, and off to the east Tabor, and snow-capped Hermon, and the Lebanon range of which it is a part. On a clear day one can see even beyond the Jordan, to the mountains on its further side, while at the very base of the great hill is the busy modern city of Haifa, with its comparatively good harbor on the bay of Acre.

A few miles further north on the bay is the interesting ancient city of Ptolemais, or Acre as it is now called, where Paul once landed, a city that has seen many ups and downs during the last 3,000 years. Here have come Greeks with their fleets, and all-conquering Romans with their mighty armies. Arabs have besieged and taken it. The Crusaders made it the chief landing-place for their armies. Here came Richard Cœur de Lion in 1191, and a few years later came the Knights of St. John, who gave the town their own name, "St. Jean d'Acre." Afterwards came the Turks and maintained possession for many years. Its modern history begins when Napoleon Buonaparte tried to take the city, but was unsuccessful, because Sir Sidney Smith and his British sailors sided with the native garrison.

Over and over again the town has been destroyed, and it was only some seventy-five years ago that the united fleets of Great Britain and Austria bombarded the devoted city, and have left the broken parapets and rusty, useless guns to tell the traveller to-day of the might of their warships.

Acre was a flourishing city in the time of our Lord, but Haifa, the important modern seaport, was not then in existence, at least as a town of any importance.

All these marvelous historic sites we can see from the top of Carmel, but we have not forgotten the event for which the mountain is chiefly celebrated. There is no more dramatic scene in all the Old Testament than that which occurred here, when Elijah summoned the Priests of Baal to the great test of the worth of their god on Carmel's top. The strange, weird scene is familiar to every Bible reader. The priests hysterically calling upon their gods in vain, cutting themselves and crying out hour after hour for the fire from Heaven, Elijah standing calmly by until his turn came to quietly pray, "Hear me, O Jehovah, hear me, that this people may know that thou, Jehovah, art God." Then in imagination we see the fire fall from heaven, and the water with which the sacrifices were drenched licked up and the burnt offering and the wood consumed and we can see the awe-stricken people falling on their faces and crying out, "The Lord, he is God! The Lord, he is God!"

As we stand here we can also see the prophet bowing himself to the earth while he tells his servant to go up to the highest point and look towards the sea. Over and over again he went, and the seventh time he saw a cloud arising out of the sea "as small as a man's hand." We know the sequel to the story, how the heavens grew black with clouds and wind and there was a great rain, and how Ahab drove off to Samaria in furious haste, Elijah running before him.

The place where these miracles are said to have taken place is now marked by the Monastery of Elijah, where a score of monks live, and where there are also accommodations for the many pilgrims who delight to climb the steep sides of Mount Carmel.

From Mount Carmel, it is most natural to believe, that the pilgrim family of our Lord on their way from Egypt would turn directly eastward, and after a few miles of weary travelling over the rugged hills, would find themselves in humble little Nazareth, whither we shall follow them in another chapter.

NAZARETH HIS BOYHOOD'S HOME

AS the Christian approaches Nazareth, he finds a homely fascination about the little city which is not shared even by Bethlehem or Jerusalem. Here Christ the boy lived and worked and studied and played. Here He helped his father in the rude carpenter's shop. Here He learned from His mother's lips the Psalms of David, and the brave words of the prophets, with which He showed Himself so familiar in after life. Here He walked back and forth from their humble home to the only spring which the town boasted then or now, holding to His mother's hand, while she carried on her head the graceful water jar, empty when going to the spring, and full to the brim when they returned, just as we see the women and the children to-day by the scores and hundreds in modern Nazareth. Here indeed we seem to come nearer to the human Jesus than in any other place.

Before He began to work His miracles, before He became famous in all the regions round about as a great teacher and rabbi, we can think of Him as a boy among boys, as a young man among young men, and tempted in all points like as we are.

Nazareth, too, has the advantage, so far as the modern traveller is concerned, of lying in the heart of a beautiful and picturesque country, a country well worth visiting for its scenic beauties were there no sacred historic associations connected with it.

The road from Haifa, at the base of Mount Carmel, where we last found ourselves, first crosses the plain of Kishon, and winds its way through fine olive groves and mulberry plantations, later following a charming valley dotted with oak trees. After some twenty miles the road begins to climb sharply, and now we have a series of magnificent views. The great Plain of Jezreel, which we shall cross in a later journey, stretches far off to the mountains on the south. Little Hermon and Mount Tabor come into view, and a great stretch of southern Palestine, green and flowery, or brown and bare, according to the season of the year, fills our eyes.

Hundreds of events recorded in Scripture have occurred on the plains or hillsides which stretch before us. Hundreds of battles great or small have here been lost or won. Millions of men, some of them among earth's greatest captains, have here lived their little lives, but while they have had their day, and left scarce a trace behind, He whose footsteps we are following from Carmel to Nazareth, still lives, while not little Palestine alone but all the world proclaims His growing might and influence.

Nazareth is peculiar in this respect, that, except

from one or two points at a distance, the traveller cannot see it until he is close upon its site. In this respect it is something like the city of La Paz, the capital of Bolivia. This city lies 12,000 feet above the sea, and yet is so hidden in a deep cleft among the Andes, which looks almost like the crater of a volcano, that one has no idea that he is close to a thriving capital of nearly one hundred thousand people until he looks over the edge of a precipitous cliff, and sees the red-tiled roofs of the city half a mile below.

So Nazareth, though high above the sea, is embosomed by the higher hills around it. Suddenly it comes into view as we ascend the Wâdi el-Emir. The first view of Nazareth, especially if we are fortunate enough to visit the little city in the springtime, is charming indeed. It has little of the squalid, mean appearance which makes many Palestinian towns of the second rate eyesores on the fair landscape. We get glimpses of olive orchards and fig trees, the evergreen cactus hedges show off well against the white walls which abound on every side, and in the fall we should find the queer, awkward, fleshy leaves of the cactus blossoming at all sorts of strange angles, with bright red and yellow fruit, deliciously cool and refreshing in hot weather, if one can but avoid the sharp thorns with which it defends itself. The long, steep climb which travellers are compelled to take when approaching Nazareth from the south or west enhances

JERUSALEM, THE MOSQUE OF OMAR, AND OLIVET IN THE DISTANCE.

AN ARCHWAY IN JERUSALEM.

GOLGOTHA, THE "PLACE OF A SKULL."

The Grotto of the Nativity.

The "Garden Tomb."

The "Wailing Place" of the Jews.

Types of Palestine Natives.

STREET VENDERS ON THE JOPPA ROAD.

DRIVERS AND DONKEY BOYS.

GENERAL VIEW OF NAZARETH.

AT THE "FOUNTAIN OF THE VIRGIN," NAZARETH.

the charm of the scene, when at last the city suddenly breaks upon the view.

Zigzag after zigzag we climb, with nothing in sight but the gaunt, treeless hills that surround the city, or the more pleasing distant view, until it seems as though the zigzags would never end. But when the last one is surmounted we forget the toilsomeness of the way by reason of the rewarding sight which has awaited us at the end of our climb.

It is true that when we actually enter the streets of Nazareth the disillusionment begins, as in all eastern cities. We do not find the city so fresh and fair as it looks from a distance. We find many foul, ill-smelling lanes which have never heard of modern sewerage or sanitary laws, but even in this respect, Nazareth compares more than favorably with most of the cities of Palestine, and the fine buildings which have been erected by Latin and Greek Christians, as well as by the Protestants, the churches, the monasteries, the hospitals, the convents and the colleges on which money has been lavishly expended, gives the place an appearance of wealth and prosperity which it shares with no other city of Palestine except Jerusalem.

I am inclined to think that this lavish expenditure of foreign money is not altogether a good thing for Nazareth, and that it may make the little town a city of paupers, such as Jerusalem has become in large measure, where every branch of the Christian Church tries to outdo the others in superfluous charities and schools, and an intense rivalry exists to get children enough to teach and work enough to do to justify their existence. It should be added, however, that neither in Nazareth or Jerusalem are the Protestants guilty of running to any excess in this matter, as are the Greek and Latin churches, whose expenditures are largely a matter of political propaganda and influence.

The various churches have their own quarters, the Latins on the south the Greeks on the north, the Mohammedans near the centre of the city. Nazareth, with its 15,000 inhabitants, is predominantly Christian, and constantly growing more and more exclusively so, while the Jews, not having any sacred associations connected with the city, are the smallest element of all.

The Protestants are represented by a hospital of the Edinburgh mission, an orphanage for girls, a church and five day schools connected with the Church Missionary Society, and a great and needed work is done in promoting a more spiritual form of worship in the midst of the dense superstition and almost fanatical idolatry of some of the other churches.

Professor Robert L. Stewart, in his admirable book about "The Holy Hills," has well said "The so-called holy places which tradition has localized here are all apocryphal, and have no claim to veneration or regard. The intelligent visitor does not come to Nazareth to see holy places, but a holy place. It is a place forever memorable and sacred, not because of one or more conspicuous events, but because it was the home of Jesus for nearly thirty years of His earthly life. Here the Holy One of God dwelt among men, and every foot of this little mountain-rimmed basin has been hallowed by His steps."

Let us take a walk together through the main street of Nazareth. We start from the modest but comfortable little Hotel Germania, on the southern edge of the town. Hardly have we stepped out of the door before our ears are assailed by post card and spurious curio venders and by girls with lace to sell, who are so unbearably persistent in their attentions as to follow us half around the town, extolling in shrill tones the excellence of their wares. Afterwards we can hardly step out on the balcony or show ourselves at the window but one of these Nazareth maidens perched on an opposite wall, will wave a yard of lace at us, and shriek out something about its rare excellence and ruinously cheap price.

However, shutting our eyes and ears, so far as we can, to these annoyances, and refusing numerous offers of importunate guides, we pick our way over the muddy streets until we see on our right an ancient threshing floor where some cattle are herded, and where our noses are assailed by a dreadful stench from the carcass of an animal long dead, and from which ravenous pariah dogs are pulling strips of rotten flesh. Day after day the carcass lies there, with no thought, apparently, in the mind of any Nazarene that there should be other scavengers than the dogs.

A Syrian hotel we next pass on the left, from whose open windows issue the metallic notes of a modern graphophone from New York, grinding out music-hall songs, and American jokes, to the apparent delight of a numerous sidewalk audience.

Soon, however, we leave these distracting sights and sounds and odors behind, and enter the door of the Church of the Annunciation, which is within the Latin Monastery. Here we see after passing through the Chapel of the Angel, a round stone column, which is called the Column of Gabriel, just inside the entrance of the Chapel of the Annunciation. Here Gabriel stood, according to the tradition of the Latins, when He told the Virgin of the Holy Child which should be born to her. A few feet away is another column, called the Column of Mary, where the Virgin is supposed to have stood. Here, the priest will tell us, was the House of the Virgin, and he will also assure us solemnly that some 800 years ago, this house was transported by supernatural power to Loretto, near Ancona, in Italy in order that it might not be captured by the Moslems. This of course satisfactorily accounts for the fact that the house is no longer on the rock where we are standing.

However, the whole house does not seem to have

JERUSALEM, FROM THE MOUNT OF OLIVES.

taken flight to Italy for the attendant next shows us what he calls the Kitchen of the Virgin, which the irreverent guide-book assures us is an old cistern.

Soon our priest-guide obtains a key and lets us into a room which he declares is the workshop of Joseph, where is now a chapel, built only about fifteen years ago, though the tradition that hallows it is some three hundred years old. On the altar of this chapel are carved these words "Hic erat subditus illis" (Here He became subject to them). Over the altar is a beautiful painting, by a French artist, of Christ in the carpenter shop.

Evidently apocryphal as are these alleged sites this quotation from the Scriptures brings us back to realities. Here, somewhere in Nazareth, Jesus the Boy lived and grew up. Here, somewhere, perhaps within a stone's throw of this very spot, Joseph had his shop, and here the obedient Son helped His father to shape the yokes and ploughshares and the smaller instruments which the farmers and the householders needed.

In those days as in these, all the houses were doubtless built of stone or mud and not of wood as in America. The carpenter was not a housebuilder, as he often is with us, but a joiner, or cabinetmaker, or a fashioner of useful tools and implements. Somewhere in this very vicinity was their humble home too, not unlike the peasant's home of to-day, perhaps built of sun-dried clay, with one or two small rooms, with no window or chimney perhaps, but only a doorway and some holes in the wall through which the acrid smoke might make its way into the outer air.

In some such place as this, doubtless, He had His early home, Who afterwards had not even so poor a place in which to lay His head.

Leaving the Latin Monastery we seek the synagogue, which for more than 1,200 years has been believed to be the place where Christ preached when He came back to Nazareth where He had been brought up, and where, as Luke tells us, "He entered the synagogue on the Sabbath Day, and stood up to read." He read the sixty-first chapter of Isaiah, words so prophetic of Himself, "The Spirit of the Lord is upon me, because He anointed me to preach good tidings to the poor."

The synagogue now belongs to the United Greeks, and further on we find a modern chapel belonging to the Latin Christians within which is a great block of hard chalk about ten feet square, connected with the tradition of the last scene of our Lord's life in Palestine, for here it is said that He came after the resurrection, and broke bread on this stone table, with His disciples.

It is a relief to leave the tawdry embellishments of these chapels with their chattering guides telling their twice-told tales, and find ourselves once more in the open air gazing at the great natural features of the scenery which our Lord must often have gazed upon, things so much more genuine and helpful as reminders of Him than any that the chapels cover.

On the west side of the town, behind the Maronite church, is a long, steep cliff, or series of cliffs, now covered with abundant rubbish which the centuries have accumulated, out of which have grown spiny cactus trees. But if in imagination we can clear these away, we find walls of rock which might once have been fifty or sixty feet high. Dean Stanley thinks that this may have been the "brow of the hill" whereon the city was built, and that here, after the sermon in the synagogue, before alluded to, where He told them that no prophet was acceptable in His own country, the people rose up in their wrath to throw Him down headlong. Others, however, place the "Hill of Precipitation," at a considerably greater distance from the city.

Of all the sites which stir the sentiments of the Christian traveller to Nazareth, none begins to equal the Virgin's Well. There has never been but one fountain in Nazareth. There is only one to-day, and to this fountain for thousands of years, have come the maidens and matrons of Nazareth, carrying great earthenware jars upon their heads, of the same identical shape to-day, doubtless, as thousands of years ago, to draw water for all household purposes. As I visited the fountain, at least a score of girls and women were gathered there at the sunset hour, with their full or empty jars. When full they would hoist them to their heads, and with erect and stately stride bear the wholesome, precious water to their homes.

In all my walks through Nazareth, in the remotest streets, I was constantly meeting women with these full or empty jars, going to or returning from the well. Some of them lived nearly a mile from the only water supply, and every day, perhaps several times a day, they must take the pilgrimage to Mary's Well, and carry the scanty gallon or two that they needed for their household meals, or their infrequent ablutions.

The source of the spring is in the crypt of the Greek Church of the Annunciation, and the water gushes from the rock in a great crystal stream that never runs dry. Past the altar it runs, and out into a cistern from which it is dipped up for the many pilgrims. Then it is conducted outside of the church, through a rock-hewn conduit, where, under a high and picturesque arch, it issues in a number of streams for the Nazarene maidens who there fill their jars. But the water has not yet fulfilled all its task, for when the water-carriers are comparatively few, it soon fills the stone tank beneath the spout, overflows it, and is carried off to irrigate the gardens and the orchards near by.

This is the one spot in Nazareth where we can seem to place our feet surely in the footsteps of the Master. Here the fountain is to-day. Here it has always been. Here, as a little boy by His mother's side, and in His

TIBERIAS, FROM THE LAKE.

FISHERMEN ON THE SEA OF GALILEE.

THE ROAD TO BETHLEHEM.

later life as well, He must often have come, and as we see the abundant crystal stream gushing out to quench the thirst of man and beast and to irrigate with its surplus the parched ground, we feel that it is a fit symbol of Him who calls Himself the Living Water, of which "if a man drink he shall never thirst."

BEYOND THE JORDAN

WE have seen that Nazareth in its rock-rimmed basin among the hills was in our Lord's time, even more than now, shut away from the great highways of travel. Nevertheless, even in those days it was not far removed from these chief roads, and the Roman capital of Galilee, Seffurieh, was but a few miles distant, so, although dwelling, during those long and quiet years, in the comparative seclusion and isolation of the little mountain village, by climbing one of the hills that surrounded the city, He could see the roads leading in various directions, over which armies with mighty generals at their head, had marched, and along which great caravans of camels loaded with merchandise from all parts of the known world were continually moving.

Not only was the ancient Roman capital near by, but the important cities of Tiberius and Capernaum, Cana of Galilee, and other places familiar to the Christian student, were not far off. These we shall visit later, but to-day we must follow our Lord into the wilderness, and to the place of His baptism and temptation, for no journey to Palestine is complete, if one has not seen the rugged, dreary, but, historically, most interesting region beyond the Jordan.

At one of the fords of the Jordan, called Bethabara, "House of the Ferry," or Bethany, as in the Revised Version, which means much the same thing, John the Baptist was preaching day after day to great throngs of people, who came from Jerusalem and from all parts of Judea, and "many were baptized by him, confessing their sins."

Jesus, knowing of this uncompromising prophet, hearing of this mighty "voice crying in the wilderness," set out from His home in Nazareth after the thirty quiet years, in which He had been preparing Himself for His redemptive mission, to find John, and to hear for Himself the message that was so arousing the people.

Robert Bird, in His graphic life of Jesus the Carpenter of Nazareth, thus imagines the young Nazarene, as He starts from His father's home on the long pilgrimage which was to end three years later on the Cross at Jerusalem. "He was dressed as a young countryman, with a long inner tunic of soft white cloth, gathered at the neck, and coming down to His feet, and over that a loose cloak of thick gray or blue stuff, to wrap around Him in cold weather. He had common winter shoes buckled on His feet and a long stick in His hand. He is tall and strong, and His step firm, as He gently supports His mother, and speaks words of consolation to her. They go by field and hedge, till a turn in the path hides them from view. A little later and the same bend of the road shows a woman's figure returning alone. She walks slowly, and her head is bent as though weeping, for she has parted from her Son, and her heart is full of fears."

Fanciful as this description may seem, it is not untrue to life, and we can also follow in imagination our Lord's journey, partly at least on the east side of the Jordan, until we come to the ford or ferry where John was preaching and baptizing. Authorities differ sharply as to the site of the Bethabara, or Bethany, mentioned in the first chapter of John. The maps in most of our Bibles place it at a comparatively short distance below the Sea of Galilee, nearly opposite to Mount Gilboa. Most travellers, however, are glad to believe that it is at the "Pilgrim's Bathing Place," much further south, and only an hour's walk north of the Dead Sea, while some of the most critical authorities place it some five or six miles to the north of this place, at the Nimrim ford, at the mouth of the Wady Shaib nearly opposite Jericho.

Though the site of the Baptism is difficult to determine with absolute certainty, we must again remember that we are seeking a sacred place, and not sacred places, and that this whole region is hallowed not only by the footsteps of our Lord as He went back and forth between Galilee and Judea, but by many another sacred scene. At one of these fords of the Jordan, Joshua led the children of Israel across it and into the promised land. Not very far away, on Nebo's lonely mountain, from whose top the goodly land of Canaan could be seen, Moses was buried,

> "And no man knows his sepulchre,
> And no man saw it e'er;
> For the angels of God upturned the sod
> And laid the dead man there."

On the plain between Nebo and the Jordan, Elijah was translated, and we hear Elisha's awe-stricken but triumphant cry ring out, "My father, my father, the chariots of Israel and the horsemen thereof!"

At another crossing place, where the River Jabbok joins the Jordan, known as the Damieh Ford, Jacob and his family, with their flocks and herds, crossed the river, and perhaps also his grandfather Abraham before him.

It was here, too, probably, that the men of Ephraim suffered their crushing defeat at the hands of the Gileadites, because their inability to give the *sh* sound told the Gileadites that they did not belong to their clan. Here is the curious story of this crossing of the Jordan as told in the book of Judges: "And it was so that when any of the fugitives of Ephraim said, Let me go over, the men of Gilead said unto him, Art thou an Ephraimite, if he said nay, then said they unto him, Say now *Shibboleth* and he said *Sibboleth,* for he could not frame to pronounce it right. Then they laid hold on him, and slew him at the fords of the Jordan, and there fell at that time of Ephraim forty and two thousand." So at this ford was coined a word which has found its way not only into our English dictionaries, but into those of most modern languages.

There were other famous fords of the Jordan, like the one between Beth-shan and Jabez Gilead, which may have been the one by which our Lord would cross the Jordan in some of His journeys between the north and the south of Palestine and possibly on this journey as well. These associations so intimately connected with the story of the Old and New Testament, make the so-called Jordan wilderness of supreme interest.

It is not by any means a desert, as some Bible readers are led to imagine, for though it is dry and barren enough, apparently, as seen under the scorching heat of the summer sun, there are pastures in these deserts for the flock, and along the banks of the streams there is often a thick canopy of verdure, the abode to-day of wild boars and jackals and in former times of fierce lions and leopards. "These wildernesses," says Rev. James Neil in his *Palestine Explored,* "abound for the most part in caves and hiding places, which render them the more insecure since such of these spots as can easily be defended, are still, as in the days of Saul, from time to time the resorts of bands of reckless and desperate outlaws. No dwelling is to be seen there for a distance of many miles, save the low black tents of almost equally lawless Bedouin Arabs, whose 'hand is against every man,' that is who are a powerful organized confederacy of robbers. No cultivation is attempted, and the bold shepherd alone, of all dwellers in town or village, frequents the spot."

This reminds us that on the edge of this desert, frequently perhaps making excursions into it to find pasturage, David kept his flock, and we cannot fully understand the unrivalled beauty of the twenty-third Psalm, until we have studied it with these desert fastnesses in view.

My readers who have seen the Grand Canyon of the Colorado on our western plains, have had an illustration, on a still grander scale, of the general topography of the Jordan region. The Jordan canyons, can not, it is true, equal in depth and majesty, or height of coloring, these magnificent gorges of the Colorado, but, in some places they approach them in their rugged sublimity, and they have been formed by the same forces of nature, the erosions of the water courses that have cut their way through the everlasting hills. Numberless ravines cleave the country in deep rock-strewn grooves in every direction.

For a distance of fifty miles, north and south, on the eastern slope of the Judean mountains, this wilderness extends, and when we reach the neighborhood of the Dead Sea we come to the most desolate part of all. Steep and ragged hills tower above us, forming a wall nearly 4,000 feet high. Not an unbroken wall, it is true, for, after rising precipitously for some 2,000 feet, until we reach practically the level of the Mediterranean, the ascent becomes more gradual, until we look down from the upper plateau to the cavernous depths where the Dead Sea lies. Exaggerated notions of the mephitic character of the waters of the Dead Sea abound in many a traveller's tale. It is not true that no bird can fly across it, or that it brings death to man or beast whose lips may touch its waters. On a smaller scale, it is much like our own great Salt Lake, and has been formed by the same processes of nature, and much of the so-called wilderness, if subjected to modern processes of agriculture, would doubtless, like Utah, blossom as the rose.

Near here David kept his flocks, and, as we have said, often made excursions into the wilderness to find fresh pasturage. One of these frightful gorges doubtless suggested to his imagination the undying expression, "The Valley of the Shadow of Death." The wild beasts that then as now made the wilderness their home, made it necessary for the shepherds to carry the staff and the rod, or the "club," as perhaps it might better be translated, to defend the flocks from the prowlers of the night.

"This club," says the author of "Palestine Explored" who has made the most careful and minute study of things Palestinian, "is a very formidable weapon in the hands of a stalwart shepherd. It is about two feet long, with a huge rounded head, into which are driven a number of heavy iron nails. It is easily attached to the shepherd's leather belt or girdle, by a noose or cord, passed through a small hole in the end by which it is grasped." No wonder it was needed, since we are told that "the shrieks of the hyena and the yell of the jackal till quite recently were heard around the very walls of Jerusalem. Fierce Syrian bears and powerful leopards prowl in the less frequented parts. . . . . Huge birds of prey with the formidable lammergeyer (the ossifrage) at their head, still hover above the desert, out of sight at ordinary times, but ready with lightning speed, to swoop down on the faint amongst the flock or even to do desperate battle on the edge of some precipice, with the shepherd himself."

No wonder the Psalmist cries out concerning the great Shepherd, "Thy rod (or club) comforts me," for it defends me from all mine enemies. The staff or crook also comforts him, for by it the shepherd points the way to the sheepfold, and by it catches by the hind leg, and keeps from danger, any adventurous member of the flock that wanders into dangerous and forbidden by-ways of the wilderness.

When the flock is scratched and torn by wild beasts

or vultures, or by the thorny shrub, he is anointed with the healing oil which the shepherd carries, and the table which is spread for him in the wilderness is the luscious green pasturage which here and there, even in the midst of these defiles the shepherd finds for his hungry flock, while, from the big wooden bowl which the shepherd carries, he gives the flock a drink of cooling water, a bowl so generous and so full that sometimes their "cup runneth over."

Thus we see with how much of the most beautiful imagery of the Bible (and the twenty-third Psalm is by no means the only one which refers to the wilderness) is our journey of to-day connected.

There is one exception to the statement that this desert region is uninhabited, for the Greek Convent of Mâr Sâbâ, clings to the cliffs of the Kidron valley "like a swallow's nest." If we have a letter of introduction, and knock loudly enough at the door of the monastery, we can get a night's lodging in this queer hostelry, though we shall find the beds infested with other occupants who have taken up their permanent lodging there.

For more than fourteen hundred years these rock dwellers and their predecessors have inhabited this cliff. We find about fifty monks there to-day. They live on vegetables, with frequent fasts to punctuate their scanty meals, and their lazy life, aside from their devotions, is spent principally in feeding the wild birds, the pigeons and the starlings which abound in that vicinity. They do not have to toil or spin to any great extent, since they are supported by their compatriots in other lands, and the little gardens which have been formed in the built-up terraces furnish them with most of the vegetables which they need.

Somewhere in this same wilderness occurred that mysterious passage in the life of our Lord, which, had nothing else happened there, would make it forever one of the most sacred parts of the Holy Land. I will not enlarge upon the vivid and succinct account given in the Gospel of Mark.

"And straightway the Spirit driveth Him forth into the wilderness and He was in the wilderness forty days, tempted of Satan, and He was with the wild beasts, and the angels ministered unto Him."

AROUND THE SEA OF GALILEE

AFTER the temptation in the wilderness, which Matthew and Luke so graphically describe, our Lord seems to have returned to the scene of John's preaching. Again the Baptist broke out in the rapturous, prophetic exclamation, "Behold the Lamb of God!" John the Evangelist and Andrew seem to have been moved by that exclamation, to follow Jesus, and soon, owing to their persuasion, Simon Peter, and Philip and Nathanael were added to the first little company of our Lord's followers, though His formal call to them to be His disciples seems to have come later, when they had all returned from the Jordan to Galilee.

We cannot follow their exact course, but the next thing that we know of their Master He is performing His first miracle, in Cana of Galilee, at a marriage feast. Hither we can follow Him to-day, for it is quite certain that the ancient Cana, is the present Kefr Kenna. We know little about the ancient town, and the present Cana has doubtless degenerated from ancient prosperity as much as have the other cities of Palestine.

To-day we find a village of a thousand inhabitants, about half of whom are Christians, and when we enter the Greek church, we are asked to stretch our credulity to the point of believing that the stone jars which are there on exhibition are the very same water pots of stone "containing two or three firkins apiece," which Jesus commanded to be filled, when "the water blushed to own its Lord."

Of course, since Nathaniel lived in Cana, our officious guide must point out the site of his house, for it would never do to neglect such an opportunity to identify the possible home of a Bible character. We find now upon the site, a little sanctuary where the Franciscans worship. We learn also that they have a school for boys and girls, and that the Greeks also have a boys' school. A not unpleasant reminder of the water that was turned into wine, we find in the shouts of the children who follow the tourist calling out "Hajji! Hajji!" (Pilgrim) and offering him a drink of water from their earthen jars.

Should we choose to go from Nazareth to Galilee by a longer route we should not pass through the traditional Cana, it is true, but we should be rewarded by having an opportunity to climb Mount Tabor, which should not be omitted in any visit. The view from the mountain is superb. The blue waters of the northern end of the Sea of Galilee can be seen. On the west is Mount Carmel, which we have already visited, while the mountain which dominates the whole scene, the snow-clad Hermon, is by far the most beautiful mountain of Palestine. The Psalmist, however, evidently considered Tabor a good second to Hermon, for in ascribing glory to Jehovah, he cries out "The north and the south, thou hast created them; Tabor and Hermon shall rejoice in thy name."

Looking to the southwest we are reminded of the story told in Judges of Deborah and Barak, of Jael and Sisera, for in full view is the battle-field where Barak defeated Sisera, and somewhere within our range of vision Jael had doubtless pitched her tent, into which she lured the defeated Sisera to his death.

For many centuries Mount Tabor has been considered to be the Mount of the Transfiguration, though modern research throws doubt on the site. However, such eminent authorities as Origen and St. Jerome thought this was the hilltop to which Jesus took Peter and James and John when "He led them up into an high mountain, and was transfigured before them."

More than twelve hundred years ago, three churches were built on the top of Mount Tabor, in remembrance of the three tabernacles which Peter proposed to build.

As we go on toward the Lake of Galilee another hill attracts our attention. It is only about a thousand feet high, scarcely more than half the height of Tabor, but its curious conformation compels the eye of every traveller, for it has two distinct peaks. This is none other than Kurn Hattin, which the Crusaders decided, when they came to Palestine, was the place where our Lord delivered the Sermon on the Mount, and also near the spot where He fed the five thousand. Well is it indeed for us that we have something more and better than the uncertain tradition that here the beatitudes were spoken, that we have our Lord's words themselves and that we do not need to visit this somewhat dubious site to know that the poor in spirit, and the meek and the merciful and the pure in heart and the peacemakers and those that hunger and thirst after righteousness are among the ones whom Jesus calls "blessed."

A ride of an hour and a half from Kurn Hattin brings us to our first view of the lake, lying far below us. It takes an hour longer to wind down the many zigzags, until we find ourselves in ancient Tiberias, on the very shore of the lake, which from boyhood to old age every Christian has particularly associated with the life and the miracles and the parables of our Lord.

Tiberias itself is now largely a Jewish city, for five-sixths of the people are Jews, who have seven synagogues, while the rest are mainly Moslems, with a very small sprinkling of Christians. The Jews, like many of those in Jerusalem, are practically paupers, living upon the bounty of their co-religionists in Europe. We can tell them by their big black hats, and others by their fur head gear, which even in the stifling days of summer, and Tiberias at that season is one of the hottest places in the world, they never discard.

This town, like most in Palestine, is a decadent descendant of an important city, for it was once the capital of the province, when, in our Lord's time, the king removed the seat of government from Suffurieh to this city on the shores of the blue Galilee. Josephus tells us that the city was built within the space of five years, and that it was finished in the year 22 of our era, only a few short years before our Lord came to make the region of Galilee His home, and the scene of His marvellous works.

If Josephus was right, the Romans of that time surpassed Americans in their speed in city building, for Tiberias was no frontier village made up of wooden shacks with false fronts, but had palaces and a theatre, a race course and many works of art, and, because the images and figures of animals were most displeasing to the Jews, who strictly observed the first and second commandments, it does not figure largely in the life of Christ. The name is only mentioned twice indeed in the New Testament, and both times by John, when he speaks of the Sea of Galilee as the Sea of Tiberias, for this imperial city gave its name to the Lake on whose border it stood.

The Lake has three names, as we know, all of which are used by Bible writers. It is called the Lake of Gennesaret, from the plain of the same name on its

Cana of Galilee.

Gethsemane and Mount of Olives, from the Temple.

A MOHAMMEDAN MARKET PLACE.

western side. It is also called the Lake of Galilee, from the province in which it is situated, and we have already seen why it was called the Sea of Tiberias. According to our English nomenclature it sounds absurd to call this little lake, which is barely thirteen miles long, by seven wide, in its widest part, a sea; for this "sea" is surpassed by a thousand fresh water lakes in the United States and Canada. But to the German it would not seem so strange, since he speaks of the small lakes of Europe as the "Genfer See," or Sea of Geneva, or the "Thuner See" when speaking of the little lake among the Swiss hills.

But the Sea of Galilee does not depend upon its size for its unique interest among all the lakes of the world, any more than Palestine itself depends upon its magnitude for its appeal to the Christian heart. Yet even the physical characteristics of this sacred lake are unique and interesting. It lies nearly 700 feet below the level of the Mediterranean Sea. It is surrounded on all sides by hills, some of which come down precipitously to the very shore of the lake, while in other places fertile plains separate them from the water's edge.

Another peculiarity of this region is the number of wadies or valleys through which the many little rivers that feed the lake flow into it from the steep mountain sides. As we sail around the lake we can count no less than eleven of these water courses, to say nothing of the valley through which the Jordan flows, the river which is both an inlet and outlet to the lake.

Sometimes the little streams that enter the lake run through a strip of fertile plain before mingling their waters with those of beautiful Galilee, and then their banks are gay with oleanders, or green with willows and marsh mallows, which often overhang the little brook so luxuriantly as to hide the sparkling water which flows beneath them. Sometimes these streams flow through dark and sullen ravines, with precipitous walls towering up on either side to nearly a thousand feet.

In the cliffs which border the Wadi el Hamam, for instance, are a multitude of caves dug out of the face of the rock, while footways connect one with the other. Here robber bands have made their homes, and we are told that about the time of Christ a large number of these robbers were besieged in these caves by Roman soldiers. "After a series of desperate struggles, they were at length destroyed or driven out by companies of soldiers let down from dizzy heights above, in great chests, strongly bound with hoops of iron. These storied caves became at a later period the favorite abodes of anchorites and hermits. At the present time myriads of wild pigeons have their nesting places in the holes and caves of these walls of rock, hence the name Wadi el Hamam, The Valley of Pigeons."*

---
* Stewart's "Among the Holy Hills."

In Christ's time, two of the villages on the northern shore of the lake were called Bethsaida, or Place of Fishing. The western Bethsaida was Philip's home, and also the city of Andrew and Peter. This, too, was the city which received Christ's scathing rebuke: "Woe unto thee, Bethsaida, for if the mighty works which were done in you had been done in Tyre and Sidon, they would have repented long ago in sackcloth and ashes."

Since our Lord's leading disciples were fishermen, and since some of His notable miracles were connected with their occupation, it is interesting to know something about the fish and fishing of the Lake of Galilee. Here we remember, the disciples, at the command of our Lord, after they had toiled all night and caught nothing, let down the net, which enclosed such a great multitude of fishes so that their boats, when they had hauled them in, were like to sink. Into the limpid waters of this lake our Master commanded Peter to cast a hook and take up the fish that first comes up, and "when thou hast opened its mouth, thou shalt find a stater, (a coin worth about sixty cents), that take and give unto them (the tax-gatherers) for thee and me."

Again, one of the last scenes in the resurrection life of our Lord upon earth was where He partook of a piece of a broiled fish which He had prepared upon the shore for His hungry fishermen disciples, as well as for Himself.

There were three ways of fishing in Galilee, methods which are common to-day, and which I have seen fishermen using a hundred times in different parts of the East; in the Bay of Naples, in Japan and China on the Riviera, and in the entrance to the Suez Canal at Port Said, for the ways of fishermen are much alike in all parts of the world. But in none are we so much interested as in the fishermen of Galilee.

The hook and line was and is one method; the cast net, which is shaped like a bag with a mouth some three feet in diameter, which is kept open by weights, until it is thrown, is another. I have seen fishermen throw this a long distance into the water, as they wade out into the shallows near the shore, and from the peculiar word used in the New Testament, *amphibleestron,* we know that this was the kind of net that Simon and Andrew were using when Jesus spoke the memorable words, "come ye after me, and I will make you fishers of men."

Then there were larger nets which the fishermen used from the side of the boat, when they found a school of fish which they wished to capture. The one hundred and fifty-three great fishes which the disciples caught were captured by such a net, a *"diktuon,"* as the name is in the Greek.

Besides these there was the great seine net, which was used chiefly at night. This is put out on the Lake, and then the fishermen row out in boats with flares of oiled rag burning in an iron cage in the bow, making a loud noise by beating old metal pans together to drive the fish toward the net. "This is the usual method of fishing away from the shore," says Dr. James Neil, to whom I am indebted for these facts, "and it can *only be done at night,* hence the great trial to their faith, in the case of those experienced Galilean fishers, who having labored *all night and taken nothing,* were bidden by the Master, *now that it was day,* to put back to the deep, and let down their great cast nets for a draught."

Such was the occupation of our Lord's chief disciples, and such was their method of gaining a livelihood from the clean waters of blue Galilee.

A WALK BESIDE THE LAKE

LET us take a walk which the Master's blessed feet must have often trodden, along the shore of the beautiful lake, in whose vicinity He spent most of the active years of His ministry.

In the last chapter we saw something of the general features of the landscape. The oblong lake nestled among the hills, which the vivid imagination of the ancients likened to a harp, thus giving it its oldest name Kinnoreth, from Kinnor, a harp, which the Greeks afterwards made over into Gennesaret. We saw the many little mountain streams rushing through the deep wadis, or ravines, which are such a marked feature of the landscape; streams that soon lose themselves in the placid lake. We saw the Jordan coming down from the north, the chief feeder of the lake, and then making its way out from the southern end, to pursue its turbulent way down to the Dead Sea, rightly receiving its name, "The Descender," for it must tumble over its rocky bed, making a drop of nearly a quarter of a mile in its short course from the Lake of Galilee, before it loses itself in the bitter lake, from which it has no escape.

We saw the fishermen, with hook and line, or dragging their nets through the clear water of Galilee, which to-day abounds, as in our Lord's time, with a multitude of excellent fishes.

But we cannot be satisfied until we have taken a walk along the shore, to see at least the sites, and the few remaining ruins of the towns where Christ performed many mighty works, and spoke most of His deathless parables.

We will not linger in Tiberias, which is the first place on the Lake that we reached in coming from Nazareth, but take the road that leads directly north to Capernaum, which has the unique distinction of being called by the sacred writer, "His own city."

At first the road winds along some little distance above the lake, giving us a view of its clear waters rippling and dimpling under the almost tropical sun, for though far from the tropics, the Sea of Galilee is so hemmed in by mountains and so cut off from the prevailing winds, that it is one of the hottest places the traveller is likely to visit.

After about half an hour we come to our first wadi, the Wadi Ameis through which trickles a little stream of brackish water. In another half hour we come to Mejdel, the ancient Magdala, where Mary Magdalene, or Mary of Magdala, was born. How much is Christian art indebted to this little town, or rather to the one woman who made it famous, so that now the face and posture of Mary of Magdala, as the great artists conceived her, is as well known as that of any historic character who ever lived!

But what do we see to-day? A hopeless tangle of thorn and grass and unwholesome weeds of many kinds, where once were luxuriant gardens and orchards of figs and pomegranates and vineyards producing the most luscious grapes. One solitary palm seems to tell of the past glory of Mary's city, and a few mud huts and an occasional little field cleared of its undergrowth for a scanty wheat harvest are the only signs of the rudest sort of civilization to be seen to-day.

At Mejdel the hills retire from the lake, leaving room for the Plain of Gennesaret, a plain about three miles long and one mile wide. Of the extreme fertility of the soil we can gain some idea from the luxuriance of the wild growth, the size of the oleanders and the willows which line the shore, and the banks of the little streams which enter the lake, but it is difficult indeed to reproduce in our imagination the Plain of Gennesaret and the surrounding towns as they looked in Christ's time.

Dr. Robert L. Stewart, who made a careful study of all this region, and who is an acknowledged authority on Palestine, says, "In the period of the Romans, Gennesaret was the focus of life and activity of one of the most thickly settled provinces of Palestine. Its towns and villages were thickly clustered on plain and hill-

DAMASCUS, OLDEST CITY IN THE WORLD.

THE MOSQUE OF OMAR, JERUSALEM.

HOUSETOPS IN BETHLEHEM.

AT "DAVID'S WELL," NEAR JERUSALEM.

"Church of the Nativity," Bethlehem.

The Tomb of Rachel.

THE RIVER JORDAN.

THE "MOUNT OF BEATITUDES."

A Palestine Beggar.

Native Types.

The Valley Where Elijah Was Fed by Ravens.

PRAYER ON THE SAHARA DESERT.

side, and every foot of the land was skillfully cultivated. With climate mild as Egypt, fitly described as 'a harmonious blending of the seasons,' with a loamy soil of unusual depth and richness, and with an abundant water supply, which was extended over every portion of its surface, it is no marvel that it was known far and wide as the Garden Spot of Palestine."

How many of the parables of our Lord throng to our memory as we take this walk, which He doubtless so often took, for though the whole Plain of Gennesaret has lost its ancient cultivated beauty, and is no longer the settled abode of man, yet the natural features are the same. The methods of cultivation, where the soil is cultivated at all, are no different, and the flowers and trees, the rocks in whose holes the foxes dwell, and the birds of the air have their nests, are still the same as in His time.

Here He saw the sower go forth to sow, scattering with prodigal hand the precious seed, which fell sometimes upon the unfruitful rock, and sometimes in the thorny, weedy grounds of which we have so much evidence to-day; sometimes it was devoured by the birds such as hover over us at this day, while some seed fell upon the fertile well-irrigated soil, of whose abundant reward to the husbandman we have such good evidence.

Here He saw the lilies of the field, perhaps the beautiful anemones which abound all over Palestine in the springtime; and from the sparrows, such as hop about us and chirp on every side, He drew the lesson of His Father's love and care.

As we again approach the shore of the lake we find that it abounds in a multitude of shells. So numerous are they in some places that it seems as though the sand itself were simply a heap of minute crustaciæ.

A short distance beyond the home of Mary of Magdala, we come to the famous Wadi el Hamam, which I have already described, and through this wadi caravans of camels and donkeys with their precious loads make their slow way from the coast to Damascus.

Another hour and we come to the ruins of Khan Minyeh, near the shore of the lake. Whether this was the site of ancient Capernaum, as some authorities declare, or whether Capernaum lay some three miles further north at the spot called Tell Hum, is not for us to determine. Baedeker confidently asserts that "the identification of Tell Hum with Capernaum is as good as certain." However, the authorities that I have consulted are almost equally divided between Khan Minyeh and Tell Hum. It matters little, so far as most travellers are concerned, for there is nothing but ruins in either place, fragmentary and unsatisfactory ruins at the best. They are less than three miles apart, and we may be certain that within this limited compass was the place to which the Master crossed from the other side of the lake, when He came to "His own city!"

What a distinction is that for any earthly town! Not even Bethlehem or Nazareth or Jerusalem is thus designated, but only the city where He spent the years of His independent manhood with His chosen disciples preaching and teaching and working the miracles which declared His divine, godlike power.

It is a cheering thought that to-day not one city alone but a multitude of towns might be called "His own city," and not only the towns where great cathedrals raise their spires towards heaven, or great institutions teach His doctrines of love to God and one's fellowmen; but, wherever there is a humble heart devoted to His service, patterning after His example, trusting in Him for strength, and deciding to do what He would like His followers to do, there we may believe is His abode. Scarcely anywhere in this wide world is there to-day a city without some faithful hearts where He abides.

Whether Tell Hum or Khan Minyeh is the site of ancient Capernaum there is nothing in either place to detain us long except the memories of the past. At Tell Hum there are the remains of a synagogue which was built of marble, but only the bases of the columns are still in their place. This is thought by many to be the synagogue built by the centurion whose beloved servant was healed by Jesus, and of whom the Jews said, as recorded by Luke, "He is worthy that thou shouldst do this for him, for he loveth our nation, and himself built us our synagogue."

The ruins of Khan Minyeh are of even less importance, and that site is chiefly famous for the remains of a once splendid aqueduct which conducted the water from the fountain of Tabighah, a mile north of Khan Minyeh, to the plain below. This spring was so abundant in its output that it was sufficient to irrigate the whole Plain of Gennesaret, but now the water, though abundant as ever, is allowed to dissipate itself so that it fertilizes but few acres of the rich soil, and only some broken arches and piers of the aqueduct which brought life and fertility to all this region in Christ's time can now be seen. This great spring was once supposed to be the scene of the feeding of the five thousand, but we have already found that that miracle is now located by many in another place.

We are glad to find that the German Palestine Society has here a little colony with a hospiz where one may find modest accommodations for a comparatively modest sum of money. Some time let us hope that Christians from other lands will settle here in larger numbers, not as paupers, relying upon the bounty of Europe and America, but as sturdy Christian agriculturalists, who may bring back the Plain of Gennesaret to something of its former fertility and beauty.

How many of the events of Bible history cluster around these few miles of lake shore between Magdala and Capernaum! On the Plain of Gennesaret our Lord spake not only the parable of the Sower to which I have already alluded, but the parables of the Tares and the Mustard Seed, of the Leaven, of the Candle which is not put under a bushel but on the lamp stand, of the Treasure hid in the earth, the Pearl of great price, and the Draw Net. In Capernaum itself he uttered the parable of the Bridegroom, of the New Cloth on the Old Garment, and the New Wine in the Old Wine Skins. At Capernaum he called Andrew and Peter and James and John. Here he healed Peter's mother-in-law, and the demoniac besides many others who were sick and afflicted and tortured by evil spirits. Here, too, He healed the paralytic who was "borne of four," who uncovered the flat roof of the house where Jesus was speaking to let down the bed before Him because the multitude thronged the door. Here, too, He healed the man with the withered hand, in the synagogue, perhaps in the very synagogue whose foundation stones are laid bare at Tell Hum to-day. Here, too, Jairus' Daughter was raised to life, the two blind men received their sight, and the dumb man who was possessed of a devil regained the power of speech.

Indeed, it is scarcely too much to say that more of the recorded words and works of our Lord were spoken and wrought here, in Capernaum, or at least on this Plain of Gennesaret, than in all other parts of Palestine together.

An hour from Tell Hum, we reach, by a very rugged and neglected path, the ruins of Kerazeh, the old Chorazin, which shares the unhappy distinction of being bracketed with Bethsaida and Capernaum in receiving the woe spoken by the Master, when He upbraided the cities wherein most of His mighty works were done, because they repented not. What an awful doom was pronounced upon Capernaum, the most favored of all! "And thou, Capernaum, shalt thou be exalted unto heaven? thou shalt go down to Hades, for if the mighty works had been done in Sodom which were done in thee it would have remained until this day."

Besides Capernaum and Magdala and Chorazin, where to-day we find some walls of ancient houses, and the ruins of an old synagogue, Bethsaida is the point of chief interest. Many students of Galilee contend that there were two cities of this name, which is not unlikely, since it simply means "A Fishing Place," and beside a lake which abounded with so many edible fish, and where fishing was one of the chief occupations, it is not strange if more than one town was called "The Fishing Place."

About the situation of one of these Bethsaidas there is little doubt, the one called Bethsaida Julius, which undoubtedly was situated just beyond the Jordan where it flows into the Lake of Galilee. Some have considered that Bethsaida was simply the little village on the lakeside which was really the port of this important Roman city that lay a mile or two beyond. But this was not in the province of Galilee, which was bounded on the east by the river Jordan, and it is supposed that there was another Bethsaida near the northern border of the Plain of Gennesaret and not far from Khan Minyeh, the supposed site of Capernaum.

There were many cities and a multitude of suburban villages in this region in our Lord's time. Dr. George Adam Smith says, "As the Dead Sea is girdled by an almost countless hedge of driftwood so the Sea of Galilee is girdled by a scarcely less continuous belt of ruins, the drift of her ancient towns."

Such was the region where the Master spent the most active years of His ministry. Here He labored and prayed. Here He taught and "spake as never man spake." Here He showed forth the mighty miraculous power given Him by the Father, and here, happily for us, Matthew and Mark and Luke and John have recorded, each from his own point of view, the Master's words and deeds. Surely no place, except it be Gethsemane and Calvary, can be holier to the Christian heart than the northwestern shore of the Lake of Galilee.

IN THE NORTH COUNTRY

WE should delight to linger long on the shores of sacred Galilee, but other places of almost equal interest beckon us northward, and we must mount our surefooted little steeds who will safely scramble over the wretched paths that lead from Tell Hum directly north to Safed, the chief town in all this vicinity. Indeed, after the wilderness that surrounds the northern side of the Sea of Galilee, Safed seems like quite a metropolis with its twenty thousand inhabitants, three-fourths of whom are Jews. It has the reputation, too, of being the most extraordinarily dirty town in all Palestine, an unsavory reputation indeed, when we remember some of the filthy places through which we have passed.

But Safed is a junction point of a good deal of importance, for from here important roads lead out in half a dozen directions, to Acre directly west, thence to Tyre, or Sûr as the name now is, to the northwest to Banias, the Cesarea Philippi of the Scriptures on the north, and to Damascus, some hundred miles to the northeast.

Perhaps over one of these roads our Lord traveled on his journey to "the coasts of Tyre and Sidon," which we are told He visited, and over this road doubtless came the people from this neighborhood who the evangelist tells us thronged around Him on the Sea of Galilee, when He taught His disciples from the little boat, and performed the miracle of the feeding of the thousands which authenticated His divine mission.

If we take the left hand road from Safed we shall reach Tyre in about eleven hours, and shall enjoy many a glorious view of mountain and valley, and, as we approach Tyre, views of the broad Mediterranean as well.

We shall also doubtless see upon our journey many other interesting sights aside from the mountains, the valleys and the sea. Indeed, everything in Palestine is interesting, because it actually reproduces for us the unchanging customs and costumes of the East. The people whom we pass upon the highway tell us at a glance of their nationality and their religion. That man with a white turban is either a Moslem or a Druse, a sect of Mohammedanism. If he wears a green turban, we know that he is, or professes to be, a descendant of the prophet Mohammed, and the number of green turbans that we see in Palestine proclaim what a mighty family is that of Mohammed.

The peasants and Bedouins, as we have seen before,

wear a cloth, often of bright colors, over their heads, bound with a rope of camel's hair. On my last visit to Palestine many of these peasants carried muskets over their shoulders, some of them of the old flintlock type, for it was during the Balkan War, and, in order to escape the draft many of their compatriots had fled to the caves in the mountains and were living the life of highwaymen, preying upon their fellow subjects until the cruel war should be over, so that every traveller felt obliged to go armed, if it were only with a stout club.

Not long before we reach Tyre we come to the Tomb of Hiram. Here was probably the "stronghold of Tyre," of the Scriptures, where its frontier garrison defended the city on the coast from marauders from the interior. It is alluded to in the book of Joshua as the "fortified city of Tyre." The archæological critics, who would throw doubt on every traditional place in the Holy Land, are not altogether willing to admit that this is the actual tomb of Solomon's ally and contemporary, though they admit that it was built by the Phoenicians, but it was undoubtedly the tomb of some great worthy of old, and is an imposing, though a rough, monument of antiquity.

A couple of hours more and we find ourselves in the once mighty city of Tyre, the city denounced by the prophets of old for its luxury and depravity, the city besieged for thirteen years by Nebuchadnezzar, and above all the city famous for the siege of Alexander, for even to the ruler of the known world, Tyre did not yield without a mighty struggle. Here St. Paul spent seven days on his way to Jerusalem with the money he had gathered for the poor saints there. Into the region of Tyre and Sidon, too, came our Lord, though we are not certain that He actually visited this famous city.

To-day this once mighty metropolis, which sent out its ships to the ends of the earth, even to far-off Britain, and established its colonies in Italy, and Spain and Cornwall, retains scarcely a shadow of its ancient greatness. Upon its desolate rocks the fishermen spread their nets as the prophet foretold, and even in all Syria I have rarely seen a filthier little city, though one would think that the abundant waters of the Mediterranean which lave its walls and its fresh breezes which continually sweep landward, might keep it pure and clean were the inhabitants so minded. There is one oasis in the dirty little town, and that is the mission compound of the British Syrian Mission, with its pleasant garden, its school and chapel, and the air of cleanliness and refinement which pervades it in every part.

We must retrace our steps, however, over the long road to Safed, and start once more for Banias, or Cesarea Philippi, as it was called in our Lord's time. In all Palestine or Syria, we can find few more beautiful situations, for it is built in a cleft of the mountains of Hermon. In this land, so much of which is dry and thirsty, Banias is made memorable to travellers by the abundance of water which gushes from the mountain side in every direction, awakening to life flowers of many hues, rich grasses and grain, and sending its life-giving moisture down to the roots of innumerable shrubs and trees.

In ancient times it was a place of very considerable importance, and was named Cesarea Philippi after Herod's son, Philip the Tetrarch. Here came the Master from his loved Galilee, and here He propounded to His disciples, as we are told in the sixteenth chapter of Matthew, the deathless question "Who say ye that I am?" We remember how Peter answered that question, the question that has confronted tens of millions of believers since, and we can hear again Jesus' memorable words when Peter said "Thou art the Christ, the Son of the living God;" "Blessed art thou, Simon Bar-Jona, for flesh and blood hath not revealed it unto you, but my Father who is in heaven." Then was Simon's name changed to Peter the Rock.

Banias is now a village so small that its fifty little houses can nearly all be encompassed by the wall of an ancient castle. But the surroundings of Banias will forever attract the pilgrim; for above it tower the snow-capped heights of Hermon. Above the modern village is a mighty structure called Kal'at en-Namrud, or Nimrod's Castle. From beneath this castle hill, out of a cavern in the rocks which have fallen down and largely blocked up its entrance, issues a splendid stream of clear water.

This is the chief source of the Jordan, and hence flows the most historically interesting river in all the world. It is indeed far from the mightiest, but none other can compare with it in its sacred associations. It is thought by many, among whom is no less an authority than Ruskin himself, that Mount Hermon was the Mount of Transfiguration, and there is much in favor of this view. The account of the Transfiguration in the seventeenth chapter of Matthew follows immediately the conversation of our Lord with His disciples, to which I have just alluded. The implication is that after six days in Cesarea Philippi, "Jesus taketh Peter and James and John, his brother, and bringeth them up into an high mountain apart, and He was transfigured before them." It is true that in these six days they would have had more than time to return to Mount Tabor, and if any one insists that Tabor was the Mount of Transfiguration we shall not quarrel with them.

But it would seem appropriate, that upon this, the mightiest mountain of Palestine or Syria, the mountain famed in song and story, the mountain connected with so much of the history of the Israelites, the wondrous scene of the Transfiguration should have taken place.

The Psalmist loved to extol its majesty and its beauty. Even "the dew of Hermon that cometh down upon the mountains of Zion," was a symbol of the blessing of Jehovah, "even life forevermore."

The mountain is something over 9,000 feet high and it is a stiff climb, requiring some Alpine ability to go up and down in one day. We can hardly believe that our Lord with His disciples would go to the snow-clad top of the mountain, but there are many smaller spurs on which the Transfiguration might have taken place.

We find that the vineyards of the people who live near the base, climb nearly one-half the distance to the top. Almond trees abound, too, on some parts of the mountain, but as we ascend the vegetation becomes scantier and scantier, until we reach the snow line, which in winter descends so far that oftentimes the road to Damascus, over one of the lower spurs of the mountain is rendered difficult by the snow drifts.

There are few finer views in all the world than Mount Hermon affords, and if one has time he should not miss the ascent of this famous mountain. From the top we see Samaria and Galilee, the Mediterranean coast for many miles, the great table mountain of Carmel; to the north the mighty plain of Damascus, indeed almost the whole of Syria, is spread out before our eager eyes.

Descending from Mount Hermon on the northerly side, we soon find ourselves on the road, or the path rather, for tolerable roads are rare in this region, that leads to Damascus. It is a long, hard journey over the mountain trail, and most travellers, doubtless, would prefer to go by rail, as they may now do either from Beyrout or from Haifa.

But, however it is reached, Damascus is well worth a visit, and can hardly be omitted from any tour of the Holy Land. I think no city in all the East has so impressed me with its charming situation and its vast possibilities as this "oldest city in the world." I can well believe the familiar story that Mohammed, climbing a hill near by, and looking down upon Damascus with its luxurious gardens, its abundant orchards, its splendid palaces, and its water courses, making the whole plain glorious in its abundant greenery, refused to go down into the city, saying, that as a man had but one paradise in store for him, he could not afford to jeopardize his chance for the future by entering this earthly paradise.

Unlike most cities of Syria and Palestine, Damascus has always been great and prosperous. It has been besieged and captured many times. It has known many rulers—Syrians and Assyrians, Greeks and Romans and Turks—but under them all it has maintained its supremacy as the greatest metropolis in all the region.

It fact, it was inevitable that a mighty city should exist here. The Abana and the Pharpar which flow through it form an oasis the like of which cannot be found in any other part of Syria. Through every part of the city, welling out in a hundred fountains, carried through a multitude of orchards and gardens, for miles and miles, these life-giving streams make the whole region glad.

There are more Scriptural allusions than to almost any other city except Jerusalem.

To Damascus came Elisha when Benhadad the king was sick; here he predicted to Hazael that he would kill his master, a prophecy which Hazael so indignantly denied at first, and so soon fulfilled.

In the first book of Kings we read about many of the political troubles of the king of Israel that centered in Damascus, and we can never forget the story of Captain Naaman and the little maid servant of his household, who was recovered of his leprosy, when at the command of the prophet, whom the little maid had recommended, he went and bathed in the Jordan.

As we compare the clear, sparkling waters of the Abana and the Pharpar with the muddy waves of the Jordan, especially in its lower courses, we do not wonder at Naaman's indignant protest, "Are not the Abana and Pharpar, rivers of Damascus, better than all the waters of Israel? May I not wash in them and be clean?"

But the greatest event that ever happened in or near Damascus occurred after the death of our Lord, who, so far as we know, never visited this ancient city. But here came His greatest disciple one hot summer day, full of wrath against the Christians, whose pre-

THE CITADEL OF CAIRO, EGYPT.

Sphinx and Pyramid.

The Edge of the Desert.

AMID THE RUINS OF LUXOR.

A TEMPLE ENTRANCE, KARNAK.

A ROW OF WONDERFUL PILLARS, LUXOR.

COLOSSI IN THE DESERT.

AMID KARNAK'S RUINED TEMPLES.

eminent leader he was soon to become. I need not rehearse the story of the conversion of St. Paul. It is the one event that makes Damascus peculiarly interesting to the Christian to-day, and, as I walked through the "Street called Straight," as I visited the alleged house of Ananias and saw the window in the wall through which it is said Paul escaped from his bitter enemies, I felt that there were few places in all the Holy Land that could arouse nobler sentiments or that were more full of important associations.

Damascus is in no sense a disappointing city, as are many historic places in Palestine. It is full of life and vigor and bustle. From its many fountains, which are as pure and abundant as in the days of Benhadad or Naaman, seem to gush ever new vitality and prosperity. Two or three railroads centre here, connecting the city with Beyrout on the one side, and with Mecca and Medina on the other, while direct communication can also be had with Aleppo on the north and Haifa on the south.

A walk through the streets of Damascus is a never changing panorama, showing all the lights and shades of eastern life. The ragged beggar, the prosperous merchant, the gorgeous Turkish officer, the poor lunatic chained to the side of some house, or, if he is allowed to go at large, rushing wildly through the street, brandishing a little bush and demanding backshish, which the alarmed tourist is only too ready to give.

The bazaars of Damascus are most interesting and varied, from the stores where the beautiful inlaid Damascene work is made by the deft fingers of hundreds of skilled workmen to the fruit bazaars, gay with all kinds of delicious fruits and vegetables, oranges and lemons, scarlet pomegranates and yellow bananas, peppers and tomatoes, almonds and figs, and everything that can be made to grow in this charming oasis.

The candy bazaar, the saddlers' market, the cloth bazaar gay with prints of every brilliant hue, which the Syrians so much admire, each has its own individual charm, even the "Louse Bazaar," the opprobrious name given to the old clothes market, is not without an interest of its own. When we get into the region of the coppersmiths and the brassworkers, the din that they make in pounding out patiently by hand their beautiful and really artistic wares is almost deafening.

A somewhat perilous incident occurred while we were visiting Damascus in 1912. As we passed through the Street called Straight, a tremendous noise assailed our ears, and soon a procession of dervishes from the Mohammedan provinces of India appeared on their way to join the Turks in "the holy war" which they were waging just then against the Balkan Christians. They were preceded by a multitude of men and boys beating drums, clapping their hands, waving banners, and shouting, "Death to the Infidel!" We took refuge in a nearby shop and the excitement was soon over, for the people of Damascus did not seem inclined to rise against the Christians.

There are many interesting sights which this chapter does not allow me to detail, like the alleged house of Naaman, and the house of Ananias where Paul received his first lesson in Christianity. Nor can we omit the Great Mosque, on whose site once stood a Roman Temple, converted into a Christian Church, called the Church of St. John, and which twelve hundred artists from Constantinople are said to have assisted in building and decorating. A terrible fire has recently devastated a large section of Damascus, but the city which has risen so many times in the past from its ashes, shows no signs of decrepitude to-day, and will doubtless exist so long as the solid world shall last.

IN AND AROUND ANCIENT SHECHEM

WE have seen that there are three principal routes leading from the north to the south of Palestine, from Galilee to Jerusalem; one following the Jordan valley, sometimes on the eastern and sometimes on the western side of the river; one following the Mediterranean coast, and one which largely follows the ridge of hills that lies between the Jordan and the Mediterranean.

We have already taken the two former journeys. Let us now return with our Lord, as He left His loved Galilee for the last time, and went down by this middle route through Samaria to Jerusalem, for, as Luke tells us, "the days were well nigh come that He should be received up."

Of all the roads that lead from Galilee to Judea, this is the most interesting for its historical and Biblical associations, and along this road, too, the views are most charming and extensive. Within a very few years the carriage road has been completed, all the way from Tiberias and Nazareth to Jerusalem. Thus the hardships of the journey have been much mitigated, for a big two-seated "American wagon" with two horses can easily make the journey in three days.

Coming down from the hills which surround Nazareth, we enter upon the long and monotonous plain of Jezreel, or Esdraelon. If our journey is after the "former" or "latter rains," the mud may be almost hub deep in some places, and it will seem to us as though our animals can never pull us through the soft muck. And yet the journey across the plain, tiresome as it is at times, is full of interest, for this is the "Great Plain," or the "Plain of Megiddo," in whose neighborhood so many Old Testament events took place.

On the west are the mountains of Gilboa near which the disastrous battle was fought between Saul and the Philistines. Here was the scene of David's lament over Saul, and his beloved friend Jonathan, a lament which is one of the classics of woe. "Ye mountains of Gilboa," he cries, "let there be no dew nor rain upon you, neither fields of offerings. . . How are the mighty fallen and the weapons of war perished!"

Here in Jezreel, near where the battle was fought, king Ahab and Jezebel had their palace, and hither Ahab fled from Carmel, when the long drought and famine were broken, after the discomfiture of the prophets of Baal. "The heavens grew black with clouds, and there was a great wind, and Ahab rose and went to Jezreel." Here, too, in Jezreel was Naboth's vineyard, and here was where the eunuchs, at Jehu's command, threw down the wicked Jezebel out of the window, and the prophecy of Elijah was fulfilled. "In the portion of Jezreel shall the dogs eat the flesh of Jezebel."

To-day the Plain of Jezreel, and all the surrounding country are peaceful enough, and in the springtime, when it resembles a great sea of green, it is a charming sight. To-day the humble husbandman drives his furrow through the rich volcanic soil where the armies of old marched back and forth and reddened it with their blood. On this Plain of Megiddo Barak and Deborah defeated the Canaanites. Here Josiah waged war against the king of Egypt, and Pharaoh Necho "slew him at Megiddo when he had seen him." Across this plain marched the Crusaders and one of Napoleon's battles was fought near by.

What a contrast to these stirring scenes of war and adventure does the Esdraelon of the present day present! In the fall of the year the slow oxen plod patiently across its wide expanse, dragging a primitive plow which is little better than a crooked stick shod at the point, while the peasant holds the handle, and occasionally prods the laggard ox with his sharp goad. But the Palestinian cattle are never spirited enough to "kick against the pricks."

For miles and miles on this wide plain one can see no habitation, or other sign of man except the ploughman in the fall, or the harvesters in the spring, for the peasants all live in villages at the foot of the hills which surround the plain, and walk weary miles every morning to their daily work.

Jenin is a wretched little village where we may spend the night; its only redeeming feature being a good hotel of the Hamburg American line. It is a well watered spot, however, and the streams nourish some orange and pomegranate groves, and the mightiest hedge of prickly cactus that I have ever seen. Its name in the Old Testament is En-Gannim and it probably deserved its poetic name of "Garden Spring" better then than it does now. It was doubtless through this place that Ahaziah, the king of Judah, fled when Jehu followed him and smote him in his chariot.

Continuing our way south, we come before long to the village of Sebastieh, the ancient Samaria, where Ahab made his capital, and before him Omri, his father. Whatever may have been the faults and crimes of these old kings, and they were many and grievous, they undoubtedly had an eye for a good location, and for delightful scenery. Indeed, I have seen few more attractive sights in all the world than the ancient hill of Samaria.

As one looks down upon it from the north, it seems to be built up in terraces, and to stand by itself in a splendid panorama of hill and valley on every side. Nor do we have to content ourselves with scenery alone, for American excavators have been at work as I have already said on the site of Samaria, and they have found not only the ruins of an old Roman city, but under this the remains of far more ancient buildings which are supposed to have been built by Omri and Ahab, and perhaps by Jehu. Here are many columns sixteen feet in height, and the authorities tell us that the "colonnade lined by these monolithic columns was twenty yards wide, and fully one mile in length," showing that Ahab's capital was no mean city.

This famous hill, which rises some 1,500 feet above the sea, is the one to which it is supposed Isaiah refers as "The Crown of Pride," when he exclaims "Woe to the crown of pride of the drunkards of Ephraim, and to the fading flower of his glorious beauty."

The present village of Sebastieh lies on the eastern slope of the hill, and is as unwholesome and dirty and fanatical as any Turkish village in Palestine.

Not far from the village is a church built by the Crusaders called "The Church of St. John," and St. Jerome, who lived five centuries after Christ, tells us that in his day there was a tradition that John the Baptist was buried there. At any rate the tradition is sufficient to enable the inhabitants to collect a little more backshish by showing us in the crypt of the church three tomb chambers, one of which they say belonged to the Baptist, one to Obadiah, and one to Elijah. The remains of their distinguished occupants are no longer to be seen, however, for the tombs are empty, and the tradition that they were ever buried there has but scanty foundation to rest upon.

Still further south we pursue our journey, occasionally passing near, or seeing in the distance, one of the singular beehive villages which are found in this part of Palestine, where not only do the houses resemble enormous hives, but the men and women and children swarm about them almost as thickly, but by no means so busy, as the bees themselves. As we journey on, it will be strange if we do not witness somewhere in our three days' journey from Galilee to Jerusalem a wedding procession or a funeral cortége. Such a procession is well described by Rev. James Neil, in "Every Day Life in the Holy Land."

"The bride is mounted on a camel and decked with orange blossoms. With her is being carried a box painted in gaudy colors, containing her simple trousseau, and also the primitive wooden cradle of the East, always in evidence on such occasions. Those who are leading her about are rejoicing in true Oriental fashion, firing off their old matchlocks, dancing, clapping their hands, and uttering the shrill, ear-piercing olooleh. . . . . It is made by rapid vibrations of the tongue against the palate, aided by a movement of the forefingers of the right hand upon the mouth. . . . . Though frequently used on joyful occasions, it is more often associated with lamentation and woe. Thus

James cries, 'Come now, ye rich, weep and utter-the-cry-of-olooleh,' and Mark tells us that when Jairus' daughter died those in the house were weeping and uttering-the-cry-of-olooleh. . . . . Our English word yell comes from this Hebrew *Yalal*."

Mr. Neil says that in his time in Palestine, a village bride was worth from one hundred to three hundred dollars, but the price has apparently gone up since the days of Moses, for in his day the purchase money of a virgin was fifty shekels of silver, about fifty dollars. He reckons Jacob's wages as worth a dollar a week (the denarius a day of the New Testament), which would make the value of the fourteen years of labor which he served for Rachel, not less than seven hundred and fifty dollars, an enormous price it will be seen, both according to ancient and modern standards.

If it is a funeral procession that we see, and that a Mohammedan one, the body will be wrapped in a white winding sheet, and will be carried forth from the home on the bier quite open to all observers. Those who precede the procession are often poor men, sometimes blind men, who constantly reiterate the Moslem creed "There is no God but God, and Mohammed is the prophet of God." (Lâ ilâha illa-llâh, wa Muhammedur rasûlu-llâh.")

As we follow in imagination the mournful procession, which perhaps we only view at a distance, we can see it going to the mosque, and then to the cemetery, where the body is always placed with its face toward Mecca, and the sexes are as strictly separated in death as in life. The ordinary Moslem graveyard, and we shall see many of them throughout Palestine, is as dismal and disreputable a place as one can find upon the face of the earth. Sometimes its hideousness is relieved by tall cypress trees, but often it is bare and unshaded, the gravestones slanting at all angles, and some of them lying prone upon the ground. Absolutely no care seems to be taken of the grounds and the monuments are stuck into the earth without any regard to permanence. The upper end of the tombstone is often carved into the shape of a turban, or fez, and the kind of a headdress shows the rank of the deceased who lies beneath.

If it is a wedding procession that we see our imagination takes us to the home of the newly married pair, when for the first time in all his life the bridegroom sees the face of his bride, for all the preliminaries of the wedding have been arranged by go-betweens, usually the mothers-in-law.

A strange sight must the bride be to Western eyes, for Mr. Neil tells us that while her dress is of the richest material, and of most brilliant pure colors, her body is equally brilliant. "Her nails, hands, arms, breasts and feet are stained with paste of henna, yellowish red or deep orange, in elegant lace-like patterns; her cheeks and lips are painted red, her eye-brows penciled so as to appear to meet. Her eyes are tinted black between the lids by a powder of smoke-black, and the skin of her face, by a peculiar process, is made smooth and shiny as a piece of polished marble." Thus is the "bride adorned for her husband." Such is perhaps the extraordinary appearance, under her draperies, of the heavily-veiled bride whom we meet in our journey from Samaria to Shechem.

Thither we must hurry without further delay, for we shall scarcely find a more interesting place in all our journeys through Palestine. The present city, now called Nablous, is situated on the side of Mount Gerizim, and is of very considerable size for Palestine, having some thirty thousand inhabitants. Few towns have a more ancient or thrilling history. Through this vale of Shechem came Abraham, and Jacob and his sons. Here Joshua made a covenant with the people just before he died, and "set them a statute and an ordinance in Shechem." Here, when Rehoboam was king, a thousand years before Christ, the capital was established for a time, and here, despising the counsel of the old men, he adopted the advice of the young men, and in his consummate folly made his little finger thicker than his father's loins, a policy that resulted in the final separation of Israel from Judah. Here Jeroboam too made his capital, and here the Samaritans, who were so obnoxious to the Jews, and who returned their hatred in full measure, established their kingdom.

In and Around Ancient Shechem

It is interesting to know that a remnant of this ancient sect still exists, though there are now only about one hundred and seventy Samaritans all told. Still they go to the top of Mount Gerizim to offer their sacrifices, to the very spot where the Woman of Samaria may have pointed as she said "Our fathers worshipped in this mountain."

But Gerizim, the mountain on which the city is built, is not the only historic mountain in the vicinity. Across a little valley stands Mount Ebal, of about the same height, and no less famous in Bible story. Gerizim was the Mount of Blessing and Ebal the Mount of Cursing, and from the sides of these mountains, to the eager, attentive people in the valley below, the blessings and the curses were pronounced as Moses had charged them, in the twenty-seventh chapter of Deuteronomy, the blessings from Mount Gerizim and the curses from Ebal. Travellers have recently proved that from certain points on these mountains the voice carries far and can be heard by a great multitude.

There are two other places which we must visit before we leave the Plain of Shechem. One is Joseph's Tomb, which lies not far from Mount Gerizim, on the road to Sychar.

About ten minutes' walk to the south of Joseph's Tomb is the most interesting historic site of all, and a well authenticated one, for here is Jacob's well. Here, tradition tells us, also, was the oak under which Joshua set up the great stone, saying "Behold this stone shall be a witness against you, for it hath heard all the words of Jehovah, which He spake unto us. It shall be therefore for a witness against you, lest ye deny your God."

Over this well the Crusaders built a chapel where formerly had been the ruins of a church, and now the Greeks have built another church on the ruins of the Crusaders' chapel. The well, or cistern, is 75 feet deep and about 8 feet across, and is partly filled with rubbish and stones.

FROM JERICHO TO JERUSALEM

WE cannot of course follow our Lord in all His journeyings during the last momentous weeks of His life after He left Galilee for the last time. He seems to have been in Perea, in different parts of Judea and in Jerusalem more than once, before the end came. It is interesting, however, to connect His words and His works with the different places which we have been visiting.

Thus we know that in Samaria, perhaps near the city of Nablous, which we have just seen, on His last journey to Jerusalem, our Lord healed the ten lepers, and here, too, He spoke the exquisite parable of the Pharisee and the Publican. Here came to him the rich young ruler, whom He loved, and who went away sorrowful because he could not meet the test which Christ imposed. Above all, we love to think of the mothers of Samaria flocking around Him with their little children, for they must have seen in His gentle face that He loved the little ones, even before He rebuked the disciples with the undying words, "Suffer little children, and forbid them not to come unto me, for of such is the kingdom of heaven."

In Perea beyond the Jordan, during this time, were spoken six parables, the parables of the Great Supper, of the Lost Sheep, of the Lost Coin, of the Unjust Steward, of Dives and Lazarus, and above all the parable of parables, which tells the story as never before or since it has been told, of the sinner turning to God, the lost son coming back to his Father's house.

But now the last journey is to be taken, from Jericho, in the depths of the Jordan Valley, to Jerusalem, on the heights above.

Jericho lies 820 feet below the sea level, and Jerusalem more than 2,500 feet above the sea, so that in less than twenty miles one climbs upward more than three-fourths of a mile. Rightly do the Scriptures speak of "going down from Jerusalem to Jericho," but our journey is in the opposite direction, a toilsome upward climb.

Jericho, our starting point, would not detain us long, were it not for its rare historic associations. It is depressing to use the same adjectives over and over again concerning these places which figure so largely in Bible history, but it is a simple truth that most of them are wretched, dirty, decayed villages; "a group of squalid hovels," our guidebook calls it. "The inhabitants, only three hundred in number, seem to be a degenerate race, on whom the hot climate has had an enervating effect."

But the climate has doubtless always been the same,

and why should it not have had the same effect in the Roman period, when Jericho was the winter residence of kings, and enriched with palaces and fine public buildings, surrounded by balsam gardens, with great fields of grain and maize and hemp stretching far around its borders. It was called the "City of Palms," so numerous were these beautiful trees, all loaded with the dates of commerce, but now scarcely one of their descendants is left to tell of the beauties of the ancient city.

It must have been a charming resort in those old days, for Mark Antony thought it worthy of Cleopatra, for whom he had conceived such a disastrous passion, and he presented it to her. In those days conquerors could do what they pleased with a city without saying to the inhabitants, "By your leave." Why Cleopatra did not appreciate her gift we are not told, but she soon sold it to King Herod, who made it his winter home; and here he died. He was not buried here, however, but in the castle of Herodium, near the ancient Tekoa to the south of Jerusalem.

It was undoubtedly for a season, such a resort, though perhaps on a smaller scale, as the French Riviera is to-day for the monarchs and notables of Europe, or such a winter residence as Palm Beach in Florida furnishes for the rich men of America.

Such was Jericho in our Lord's time, for it had not then begun to decay, and even for centuries later it was a city of importance where councils of the church were held.

To-day it is about as barren of interest as any spot in Palestine. The ruins of an ancient church are there and a kind of tower, which probably dates from the Middle Ages, and which is said to be built on the site of the house of Zaccheus. For some centuries the sycamore tree into which Zaccheus climbed was shown as one of the curiosities of the place, but for more than a thousand years the inhabitants have not ventured thus to impose on the credulity of travellers.

The people of Jericho seem to have degenerated as much as their city. Many of them are thieves, and we are advised to keep a tight grip on our valuables, while others try to extort a few paras from the traveller by singing and dancing and clapping their hands as they keep time with the movements of their feet.

Again we must look beyond the sordid present, through the ever-ready telescope of the imagination, to the days of the splendor of this decayed town, to the time when our Lord walked its streets, when Zaccheus wrung taxes from the unwilling peasants, until he heard, in the sycamore tree, his Lord's summons: "Make haste and come down, for to-day I must abide at thine house."

Here, too, or on the roadside near by we can hear Bartimeus calling out, "Thou Son of David, have mercy on me!" mercy which was so readily and promptly bestowed. Here, too, we can hear the Master speak the Parable of the Pounds, and the glad words, applied to so many a faithful Christian since, "Well done, thou good and faithful servant!"

Thorns and briars and prickly shrubs now largely occupy the ground which produced fruits and flowers in the time of Christ, and returned to the husbandman his seed increased a hundred fold.

We have already in these journeys visited the Jordan and the Dead Sea, which lie an hour or two further on from Jericho, so we will not go further in their direction, as most travellers do from Jericho, but, with the Master, will turn our steps towards Jerusalem. It is a steep and rugged climb, though much easier than a quarter of a century ago for then 800 men were set at work to fill up the gaps in the old road which had been washed out by the floods, and to clear out the rocks with which centuries of neglect had filled the road, which in the days of Christ had been a splendid thoroughfare.

The civilization of a people may be largely gauged by its highways. The Romans were great road builders; so are the English, the French and the Swiss, and indeed all the highly civilized nations of to-day. America is making great strides in covering her vast territory from ocean to ocean with good roads, but in the Turkish domains the low grade of civilization is nowhere more evident than in the horrible condition of most of the highways. But even here things are improving, as the road between Jericho and Jerusalem indicates.

A short time after we start on our upward journey, we come to the excavations of the German Oriental Society which a few years ago unearthed the palace of Herod. The valleys, and the courses of the torrent down the mountain side, furnish the only practicable means of descending the Judean hills to the Jordan valley, and of these the road to-day, as in ancient times, has taken full advantage.

We see few signs of the habitation of man on the way. A couple of ruined houses show the sites of some ancient defenses of the road. The Monastery of St. George is built in a cavern of the rock on the left hand side as we ascend. Now and then we look into a deep shuddering gorge, like the Wadi el-Kelt which we are sorry recent archæologists will not allow us to identify with the Valley of Achor, or the Brook Cherith, where Elijah the Tishbite hid himself, and where the ravens brought him bread and flesh morning and evening.

In former days, travellers were allowed to think that they were viewing the very spot of Elijah's hermitage, but now the iconoclastic critic has robbed them of this satisfaction.

About half way to Jerusalem we come to the Khan Hathrûr, where we can refresh ourselves for the rest of the journey if we desire. It is at least refreshing to the spirit to recall here the story of the Good Samaritan, which is localized at this point, and as well at this point as any other, for the region is a sterile and gloomy one, and it can easily be imagined that here the traveller would fall among thieves. Though it happened many years ago, the story is still told, how at this point Sir Francis Henneker was set upon by robbers and left for dead by the roadside like the man in the parable.

"The bold projecting crags," says a traveller describing the road, "the dark shadows in which everything lies buried, below the towering heights of the cliffs above, and the forbidding desolation which everywhere reigns around, seem to tempt the robbers and murderers."

But the road is now entirely safe, and this we must credit to the Turkish government, which, with all its deficiencies, gives the traveller in Palestine much to be thankful for; furnishing guards when necessary in dangerous places, and above all preventing disorder and bloodshed in sacred spots like Bethlehem, and the Church of the Holy Sepulchre in Jerusalem, between the Latin, Greek, Coptic and Armenian Christians, who would shamelessly fight for their possession, and exclude all other Christians from the holy places, did not some neutral power keep the peace between them.

Ascending wadi after wadi we come at last to Bethany, a village which now contains, so far as we know, not a single Christian inhabitant, and which is about the most filthy and degraded village that occupies the site of any of the holy places of the Holy Land. It seems a sacrilege indeed that the best-loved home of Jesus, where Mary and Martha lived, where Lazarus was raised from the dead, where the woman with the alabaster vase of ointment poured it upon Jesus' head, should now be a place so mean and poverty-stricken. Forty or fifty little hovels are found among the ruins of former days, where in the days after our Lord churches and monasteries were erected in His honor. Ragged children run out from holes in the rocks demanding backshish, and offering to show us the tomb of "Lazaroos," as they call him, or the House of Mary and Martha.

To visit the tomb of Lazarus we go down a long flight of steps into what was formerly a rocky cavern, undoubtedly an ancient burying place. If it was not at this very spot, it could not have been far from here that the pathetic scene of the Gospel narrative was enacted, and that He who was so soon to die and rise again called Lazarus from the grave.

A few steps from the tomb is an ancient tower now in ruins, called the House of Simon the Leper, where as we have seen Jesus was anointed by Mary when He spoke the prophetic words, "She hath done what she could." "Wheresoever this Gospel shall be preached throughout the whole world, that also which this woman hath done, shall be spoken of for a memorial of her."

A hundred feet beyond the alleged house of Simon the Leper, stands the traditional house of Mary and Martha, and not far away a Greek chapel is built over the "Stone of Meeting," as it is called, where Martha, according to the Scripture narrative, "when she heard that Jesus was coming, went and met him, but Mary sat still in the house."

Our journey is nearing its end, for Bethany is on the lower slopes of the Mount of Olives, and as we wind up the rugged path which leads to the summit of this most sacred of all hills, we soon come to the turn of the road where Jerusalem breaks full upon the view. Not far from this spot we may well believe that our Lord, gazing upon the splendid city of old, which was so soon to be destroyed, uttered those heart-breaking words, "O Jerusalem, Jerusalem, that killeth the prophets and stoneth them that are sent unto her! How often would I have gathered thy children together, even as a hen gathers her chickens under her wings, and ye would not!"

At this point, so pathetic in its associations, so glorious in its outlook, we may well draw our story of Palestine to an end. Here we can see every place connected with the last days of our Lord's Life upon earth.

We are standing on the sacred Mount itself, which the Master so often crossed in going back and forth, from the home in Bethany to Jerusalem. There is no spot in all Palestine, I believe, that retains so completely its ancient appearance. Gnarled old olive trees still dot its sides. The churches and convents of the Russians, the buildings of the Latins and the Armenians, the Church of the Lord's prayer, erected, it is said, on the spot where the Master taught His disciples to pray, and wherein is inscribed on marble tablets in nearly forty languages the Pater Noster:—these buildings are all there, but they do not intrude themselves upon one's vision. The features of the Mount of Olives that fill the eye are the rocky, water-seamed hillsides, the olive trees and the occasional spots of verdure, which could not have been very different in Christ's time.

And there, before us, is Jerusalem, shrivelled and decadent, it is true, but the very city over which the Master wept. Below us we can see the Garden of Gethsemane, and the steep path by which, on the supreme day in the world's history, Jesus and the disciples climbed to the Prætorium, where his enemies put upon Him the crown of thorns and the purple robe. A little beyond, after He had trod the Sorrowful Way, is the Place of the Skull where "He died to save us all." Behind us is Bethany, the scene of the Ascension, where, when He had blessed His disciples, "He parted from them and was carried up into heaven."